Polish Armies 1569–1696 (1)

Richard Brzezinski · Illustrated by Angus McBride

Series editor Martin Windrow

First published in Great Britain in 1987 by Osprey Publishing,
Midland House, West Way, Botley, Oxford OX2 0PH, UK
44-02 23rd St, Suite 219, Long Island City, NY 11101, USA
E-mail: info@ospreypublishing.com

Transferred to digital print on demand 2010

First published 1987
13th impression 2006

Printed and bound by PrintOnDemand-Worldwide.com, Peterborough, UK

A CIP catalogue record for this book is available from the British Library

ISBN: 978 0 85045 736 0

Series Editor: Martin Windrow
Filmset in Great Britain

Artist's Note

Readers may care to note that the original paintings from which the colour plates in this book were prepared are available for private
sale. All reproduction copyright whatsoever is retained by the Publishers. All enquiries should be addressed to:
Scorpio Gallery
PO Box 475
Hailsham
E.Sussex
BN27 2SL
UK
The Publishers regret that they can enter into no correspondence upon this matter.

Acknowledgements

The author would like to thank the following institutions: *In England*: British Library; Polish Social and Cultural Centre, and Polish
Institute, London. *In Poland*: Polish Army Museum (MWP), Royal Castle, Central Archive of Past Acts (AGAD), University of Warsaw,
National Library, Wilanow Palace, and Polish Institute of Art, all in Warsaw; Kórnik Castle; Goluchów Castle; Royal Castle and
Czartoryski Museum, Cracow; Gdansk Provincial Archives; Gdansk PAN Library. *In France*: Polish Library, and Bibliothéque Mazarin,
Paris; Château de Sassenage. *In Belgium*: Royal Library, Brussels. *In Sweden*: Royal Armoury, Royal Army Museum, and Riksarkivet,
Stockholm. *In Austria*: Heeresgeschichtliches Museum and Kunsthistorisches Museum, Vienna; Benediktinerstift, Melk.
Special thanks to: Andrzej Dzięciolowski, Kasza Rokosz, Nick Sekunda, Gillian Byrne, Ron Poulter, Mgr. Jerzy Teodorczyk, Arne
Danielsson, John Rohde, and Felicia Tarr.

Dedication
To Hammurabi

FOR A CATALOGUE OF ALL BOOKS PUBLISHED BY OSPREY
MILITARY AND AVIATION PLEASE CONTACT:

Osprey Direct, c/o Random House Distribution Center,
400 Hahn Road, Westminster, MD 21157
Email: uscustomerservice@ospreypublishing.com

Osprey Direct, The Book Service Ltd, Distribution Centre,
Colchester Road, Frating Green, Colchester, Essex, CO7 7DW
E-mail: customerservice@ospreypublishing.com

www.ospreypublishing.com

Introduction

Although Poland's recent problems have captured the imagination of the Western world, few people will realise that at one time the Polish state was one of Europe's great powers. One of the chief instruments of her success was undoubtedly her army, which though small can claim many accomplishments and major successes in the 16th and 17th centuries.

Many will know of King John Sobieski, whose legendary 'winged' hussars saved Vienna from the menace of the Turks, but little concrete material has ever been published in the English language on the army that achieved this and other equally remarkable feats.

Who, for instance, has heard that a Polish army once took Moscow and placed a Polish Tzar on the Muscovite throne? For a long time the balance of power between Poland and Muscovy could have tilted either way, and it was only by chance that Muscovy rather than Poland 'gathered up the Russias' to become the great Eastern European power. Who realises that one of the world's great commanders, the Swedish King Gustavus Adolphus, spent most of his military career fighting the Poles—with only limited success—and based many of his reforms on his experiences against the Poles?

Indeed the Polish army had many far-reaching influences on the development of Western armies, and was an important channel for the passing of Eastern military science to the West. The Polish army can claim to have introduced the uhlan lancer; and certainly had an influence on the hussar dress usually credited to Hungary. Through her close connections with the French court, Poland exerted other influences on the development of military uniform in the West, particularly on the long-cut jackets, grenadier caps, and dragoon uniforms of the 17th and 18th centuries. Wieslaw

Stefan Bathory, Prince of Transylvania and one of the most highly regarded of Polish kings (1576 86). He wears a bright scarlet fur-lined *delia* with decorative falling sleeves; under this, a tan and red patterned silk *zupan* with turnback cuffs of Eastern style; yellow ankle boots, and a black *magierka* Hungarian felt cap. Copy of a portrait by Marcin Kober, 1583. (Polish Army Museum—hereafter MWP)

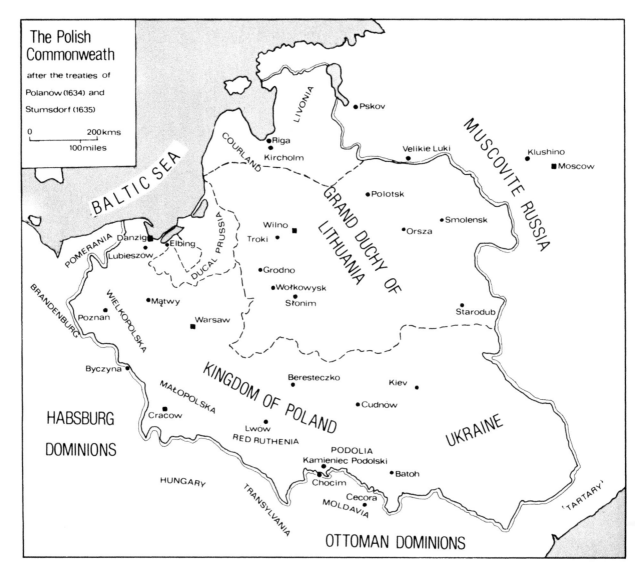

The Polish
Commonweath

after the treaties of
Polanow (1634) and
Stumsdorf (1635)

0   200kms
100miles

Majewski has even suggested that the modern divisional system had its origins in Poland via Luxemburg's teacher, the great Conde, a friend of Sobieski's wife Marie-Casimire.

Even ignoring its achievements, the Polish army of this period—with its unique blend of East and West, its colour and unique character—is a fascinating subject within its own right.

I have chosen the period from 1569 (the Union of Lublin) to 1696 (death of Sobieski) simply because it covers the heyday of the Polish hussars. To go much earlier would involve treatment of fully armoured Western-style knights; while to continue after the Elector of Saxony, August II, became King of Poland in 1697 would bring in the complication of the Saxon army.

This first title deals with the 'Polish Contingent' of the army, which includes the hussars, *pancerni* 'cossacks', and Hungarian-style infantry. The second title will discuss mainly the 'Foreign Contingent' of the army, Tartars and Ukrainian Cossacks, and other mercenaries in Polish service. This is not a straightforward division by nationality, since the 'Foreign Contingent' was for the greater part of the 17th century full of Poles, despite its name. There will be considerable overlap between the two books which are intended to be consulted together.

Much of the material presented here is previously unpublished even in Poland, and is based on research from primary sources, archives, and museums throughout Europe, and on the mountains of Polish literature on the subject. Most valuable of all have been the works of Zygulski

Rembrandt's famous 'Polish Rider': a source of much speculation, and often mis-labelled as an officer of the 'Lisowski' cossacks. Chrościcki (*Ars Auro Prior*, Warsaw 1981, p.441+) has finally identified it as a portrait of a Lithuanian nobleman, Martin Alexander Ogiński. From 1651 Ogiński was in military service. The portrait was painted in 1655 while Ogiński was studying in the Netherlands. The date of 1655 coincides with the devastating Swedish invasions, and suggests that Ogiński had the portrait painted on the eve of returning to his unit. He reached the rank of *pulkownik* in 1657, and later became Voivode of Troki, and Grand Marshal of Lithuania.

His long coat is the *zupan* often worn beneath armour. When in the West, Poles usually adopted Western dress and hairstyles (as here) to avoid being laughed at for their unusual Eastern manners. (Frick Collection, New York)

Bocheński, Górski, Wimmer, Baranowski, Kotarski, Gembarzewski and Stefańska. It is impossible in a book of this size to quote all sources and discuss all arguments, and many statements are inevitably generalised. A short list of suggested reading will be given at the end of Part 2. In the meantime, interested readers would do well to read Volume 1 of Norman Davies' brilliant and entertaining history of Poland, *God's Playground* (London, 1981).

The Polish-Lithuanian Commonwealth (*Rzeczpospolita*)

Relations between the Kingdom of Poland and the Grand Duchy of Lithuania were brought closer by the accession of the Lithuanian Vladislav Jagiello (Jogaila) to the Polish throne in 1386. Lithuania had captured vast territories stretching deep into modern European Russia, but was increasingly finding that it could no longer cope with these on its own. The only place to which Lithuania could turn

Hussar officer on a 'painted' horse. The dye is shown by the artist of the roll as bright red, although in practice the colour was probably a paler brick-red hue. From the 'Constantia' or 'Stockholm Roll' painted to commemorate the ceremonial entry of the Polish Queen Constantia of Austria into Cracow in 1605. (Royal Castle, Warsaw)

for help was Poland. On the condition that the Ukraine was ceded to Poland, the two states were formally united in 1569 at Lublin in a union resembling that of England and Wales. In this way Poland took on the duty of protecting the Eastern expanses of Lithuania—a task which was to have a significant effect in the orientation of Poland away from the West.

Together, the lands of Poland-Lithuania stretched from the Baltic almost to the Black Sea, and from the Holy Roman Empire to the gates of Moscow. In 1634 after the treaty of Polanów, when they were already past their greatest extent, they covered an area close to one million square kilometres—the largest territory in Europe, slightly larger than European Muscovy and nearly double the size of France. With a total population of 11 million, Poland-Lithuania was Europe's third most populous state after Muscovy and France.

The territory of Poland-Lithuania was one vast plain: only in the south, along the Carpathian Mountains, was there an appreciable area of uplands. Cutting across the plain were several major rivers, the most important being the Vistula, Neman, and Dnieper. These rivers and associated tributaries made transport very difficult, parti-

cularly along the line of marshes marking the Polish-Lithuanian border, which meant the two states were virtually cut off from each other in the summer. For this reason many campaigns into Muscovy did not get under way until winter, when the freezing of marshes and rivers made transport much easier.

The kingdom of Poland (usually referred to as the 'Crown') and the Grand Duchy of Lithuania were governed by a single body, the *Seym*, to which both states sent representatives. Their territories were divided into *województwa* (palatinates), each governed by a *wojewoda* (voivode). *Ziemie* (lands), *powiaty* (districts), fortresses and towns were governed by a castellan or by a *starosta* (elder). Below these were a multitude of lesser titles: chamberlain, sword-bearer, cup-bearer, etc., many of them merely sinecures. Hereditary social ranks (such as duke, earl, etc.) were banned in Poland, so these titles took on a special meaning, and had the same status as Western hereditary titles without offending the egalitarian ideals of the Polish nobility. Only in Lithuania were some hereditary ranks retained as one of the conditions of the Union of Lublin. The famous Radziwill family, for instance, used the title *ksiąze* (duke)—though the award of the rank of 'prince' to a member of the family by the Austrian court led to screams of outrage when he attempted to use the title in Poland.

Poland had an unusually large nobility: ten per cent of the total compared with one to two per cent in the rest of Europe. The wealth of these noblemen varied hugely; but all, from the richest magnate to the poorest farmer, living in conditions as miserable as the peasantry, considered themselves equals. The Polish state was set up to serve the Polish nobleman: within it he had all the freedom he could wish for, so much so that visitors such as Sobieski's one-time English doctor Bernard Connor remarked: 'Had we in England but the third part of their Liberty, we could not live together without cutting one another's Throats'.

Military Dress and Fashion

The nobleman's dress was worn virtually unaltered both at home and for war; and many of the fashionable items, such as swords and horse furniture, would be common to both. The adoption of foreign items of clothing during long campaigns abroad, often in conscious imitation of the enemy's dress, was the main influence on Polish fashion. A contemporary writer remarked, for example, on the rapid changes in dress throughout Poland in the space of only ten years, with Muscovite, Swedish and Turkish features each predominant in their turn after the return of armies from wars in these parts.

Noble dress was extremely expensive; and silks, satins, and velvets were not restricted to civilian use. For cavalry of the Polish model there was little in the way of centralised distribution of dress: men had to supply their own clothes, and they showed little restraint in displaying their wealth. The military theorist A. M. Fredro advised that lavish costume should not be brought into the camp. On his arrival in Poland King Bathory was shocked by the quantity of gold and silver being worn in the Polish army. Numerous laws were passed against sumptuous dress; but they failed to stamp out the love of splendour, and such items were widely worn on military service, particularly by the Levy of the Nobility.

Items of dress are often said to be of 'Turkish pattern' or 'Hungarian style'. These can sometimes be controversial, since it is difficult to determine the exact origin of any particular item: in Poland something might be called 'Turkish' while in Turkey it was known as 'Polish'. To complicate the problem even further, a term used for a particular item in one country often indicated an entirely different thing in another.

For a large part of our period, Hungarian dress was dominant; indeed, it is often difficult to distinguish between Hungarian and Polish styles. Some historians have suggested that King Bathory introduced Eastern and, particularly, Hungarian dress into Poland after his election in 1576; however, by the end of the Jagiellonian dynasty in 1572 most of the army and the nobility were already dressed in Hungarian style. Indeed, it seems more likely that the proliferation of Hungarian dress and custom had an influence on Bathory being elected in the first place.

Hungarian dress in turn owed a great deal to Turkish and Persian influences, and these also fascinated the fashion-conscious in Poland throughout the period. Numerous contracts were carried

Hussar armour, *c.*1540–70. Note that the mail is of a type known as *bajdana*, made of especially large rings. The pointed Eastern-style *szyszak* helmet has yet to evolve into a typically Polish style. Circular metal shields, some with fringed edges, were used as well as wing-shaped shields. (MWP)

out in Istanbul for Polish patrons, but these alone could not satisfy the huge demand. Many workshops opened up in Poland, staffed largely by Armenian craftsmen making weapons and other items in Turkish style.

The appearance of Poles abroad, especially on missions to the West, caused reactions varying from ridicule to sensation: Cossack and Tartar hairstyles that would put many a modern 'punk' to shame, eagle- and ostrich-feather 'wings', cloth-of-gold, precious silks—even solid gold and silver horse-shoes, fastened loosely to ensure that they would fall off conspicuously during ceremonial entries! City populations turned out *en masse* to witness these splendid processions; and even the ever-fashionable ladies of Paris designed themselves new costumes in the fear that they would be outshone by the splendid dress of the Polish delegations.

Kings of Poland

Sigismund II August	1548–1572
Henry Valois	1573–1574
Stefan Bathory	1576–1586
Sigismund III Vasa	1587–1632
Vladislav IV Vasa	1632–1648
John Casimir Vasa	1648–1668
Michael Korybut Wiśniowiecki	1669–1673
John III Sobieski	1674–1696

Hussar armour, c.1580–1610. The cuirass is derived from the Italian *anima*-type breastplate, constructed of horizontal lames. It is worn over a mail shirt, with a *kapalin* helmet, and leopard skin. (MWP)

The death of Sigismund August in 1572 brought to an end the great Jagiellonian dynasty. Thereafter Polish kings had no hereditary rights, and were elected by the nobility. The first elected king was Henry Valois, a Frenchman whose rule in Poland lasted barely 118 days before he ran away to take the throne of France as Henry III. His successor, Stefan Bathory, Prince of Transylvania, was followed by the three much under-rated kings of the Swedish Vasa family: Sigismund, and his sons Vladislav and John Casimir. Their claims to the Swedish throne were a major excuse for the Swedish wars of this period. The ineffectual Pole Michael Wiśniowiecki was succeeded in 1674 by John III Sobieski (actually crowned in 1676), another Pole, whose reign was marked by his almost obsessive preoccupation with the Tartars and Turks. The King of Poland, in this period, was always simultaneously Grand Duke of Lithuania.

Chronology

1558–82	**Livonian War**, against Muscovites under Ivan the Terrible.
1569	Poland and Lithuania joined as one state by Union of Lublin; Ukraine transferred to Poland.
1576–78	Rebellion of Danzig; Danzigers defeated at Lubieszów (1577).
1579–82	King Stefan Bathory's successful campaigns against Muscovite fortresses of Polotsk (1579), Velikiye Luki (1580) and Pskov (1581).
1587–88	Archduke Maximilian enters Poland to accept the crown offered by one faction. He is defeated and captured at Byczyna (1588) by Jan Zamoyski.
1598	Unsuccessful expedition of Sigismund III to recover his Swedish throne. He is defeated by Duke Charles, and deposed.
1600	Jan Zamoyski's expedition to Moldavia.
1600–11	**Polish-Swedish War in Livonia** Brilliant victories at Kokenhausen (1601) and Kircholm (1605).

1605–09	Polish intervention in Moscow's 'Time of Troubles'.
1606–09	Rebellion of nobility under Zebrzydowski. Battle of Guzów (1607).
1607	Stefan Potocki's expedition to Moldavia.

1609–19 Russo-Polish War

1609–11	Smolensk falls to the Poles.
1610	Zólkiewski defeats Muscovites at Klushino, opening road to Moscow; Poles garrison Kremlin; King Sigismund's son Vladislav becomes Tzar.
1612	Poles ejected from Moscow; Michael Romanov becomes Tzar.
1619	Peace of Devlin with Muscovy.

1614–21 Polish-Turkish War

1615	Expedition to Moldavia.
1620	Hetman Zólkiewski killed by Turks when his army disintegrates at Cecora (*Tse'tsora*).
1621	Ottoman invasion halted by Poles and Cossacks at Chocim (*Ho'cheem*).

1617–29 2nd Polish-Swedish War. Gustavus Adolphus advances down Baltic coastline.

1627–29	Hetman Koniecpolski fights Swedes to a standstill in Prussia; Gustavus wounded on several occasions. Truce of Altmark (1629).
1633–35	Ottoman invasion halted at Kamieniec Podolski.
1635	Peace of Stumsdorf with Sweden: Swedes return Prussia to Poland.

1632–34 Russo-Polish War. Smolensk is relieved, but in Peace of Polanów, King Vladislav abandons claims on Moscow.

1638–48	'Golden Peace' in the Ukraine.

1648–54 Cossack Rebellion under Bohdan Chmelnitsky.

1648	Polish armies defeated at Zólte Wody, Korsuń and Pilawice.
1651	Poles destroy huge Cossack army at Beresteczko.
1652	Cossacks wipe out Polish 'Quarter' army at Batoh.

1654–67 Russo-Polish Wars. Tzar Alexis invades Lithuania. Smolensk, Kiev and Wilno fall. Alexis proclaims himself Grand Duke of Lithuania.

Winged Hungarian/Polish hussar fighting a winged Turk. The wing was not restricted to Poland: in its earlier forms it adorned the shields and horses of riders in much of 16th-century Eastern Europe. Woodcut from Adam Czahrowski's *Rzeczy Rozmaite . . .*, 1598 (PAN library, Kórnik)

Hussars from Gostomski's troop, 1605. They carry uniform two-tailed red lance-pennants, bearing snake-like emblems and Gostomski's quartered coat of arms in a green wreath, on a red/white striped lance. The troop standard is of similar design, but larger. Hieronym Gostomski, Voivode of Poznań, was a close supporter of King Sigismund III, so it is not surprising that his private units figure prominently on the Constantia Roll. (Royal Castle, Warsaw)

1655–60	**1st Northern War.** Struggle for supremacy in the Baltic involving Sweden, Poland, Brandenburg, Denmark, Austria, Transylvania and Muscovy.
1655	The 'Bloody Deluge': Swedes under Charles X overrun Poland.
1656	Nationalist revival traditionally centred on Częstochowa monastery. Two three-day battles at Warsaw.
1657	Transylvanian invasion under Rakoczy quickly defeated.
1657	Treaty of Wehlau: Brandenburg is bought off by being given control of Ducal Prussia.
1658–9	Czarniecki's campaign in Denmark.
1660	Peace of Oliva with Swedes.
1660–61	Cudnów campaign; Muscovites driven out of Lithuania.
1661–3	Revolt of army demanding back-pay.

1665–6	Lubomirski Rebellion; battle of Mątwy (1666).
1667	Ukraine partitioned between Poland and Muscovy at Andrusovo.

1671–99	**Polish-Turkish Wars**
1672	Kamieniec Podolski falls to Turks.
1673	Sobieski defeats Turks at 2nd Chocim.
1675	Battle of Lwów.
1676	Battle of Zórawno.
1681	Podolia returned to Poland; Ukraine accorded special status.
1683	Sobieski, commanding combined Polish/Imperial army, relieves Vienna. Turks defeated even more conclusively at Parkany.
1686	Sobieski's abortive expedition to Moldavia.
1699	Treaty of Karlowitz between Poland, Austria, and Turkey.

(There is insufficient space here to list every campaign and war in this period, particularly the numerous Cossack revolts and Tartar raids: indeed, outside of the 'Golden Peace' of 1638–48, there was hardly a year in which a Polish army was not in action.)

Organisation and Recruitment

The Polish army was raised by several methods. The soldiers, however, were organised and equipped on lines which were largely independent of their source.

The peacetime standing army was developed from the *Obrona Potoczna* or 'Continuous Defence' force, used mainly to guard the south-eastern regions of Poland against raiding Tartars. In 1562/3 this became the *Kwarciani* or 'Quarter' army, so called after the fraction of the Royal revenues which were reserved for maintaining them. They numbered about 3,000–5,000 mainly lightly armed cavalry equipped with a high proportion of firearms. After the destruction of the *Kwarciani* at Batoh in 1652 the institution was abandoned and replaced by a more general system, based on the so-called *Komput* (hence 'the Computable Army'), which could be more easily expanded in time of war, and which was organised on a territorial basis.

In time of war the size of the standing army could be expanded hugely, by increasing the size of existing units and by raising additional formations of paid soldiers, although it was usually only with great reluctance that the Seym approved the funding of forces large enough for the task at hand.

Other permanent forces in Poland were the garrisons of several strategic forts; the armies of the cities; private armies belonging to the wealthier magnates; and the Royal Guard, which was in effect the king's own private army. (These will be dealt with in the forthcoming second *Men-at-Arms* title.)

'District soldiers' were occasionally raised after 1613–19. These were paid soldiers raised for short intervals on the basis of decisions by regional *seymiks*. Their chief purpose was to maintain the law during the often long periods between the reigns of the elected kings, and to provide immediate local cover against raids, invasions and civil disturbances. Organisation of units differed little from those of the rest of the army.

Peasant levies could be raised from royal estates on a semi-permanent basis at minimal cost to the state: the *Wybraniecka* infantry, and *Lanowe* and *Dymowe* (literally 'acreage' and 'chimney') levies raised in the 17th century to supplement the Wybraniecka levies. These were in effect a 'human war-tax' for a certain number of acres of land or, in towns, a number of houses (i.e. chimneys). In towns the duty was to provide an infantryman; in the countryside, where horses were more readily available, a fully equipped mounted man. Often a payment in cash was preferred, and certain provinces paid all their dues in cash. These levies were quite often dispersed among regular units.

Aside from regularly organised and paid soldiers, unpaid volunteers and local peasantry also played a vital military rôle. Units of volunteers were often raised by adventurers, such as the famous Aleksander Lisowski. These received no pay, and were not usually included on any registers, but were given the right to keep any booty that came their way with no questions asked. Poorly disciplined, they often proved more trouble than they were worth; but they left behind them a trail of destruction that few enemies could ignore. *Ad hoc*

Hussar unit on the Constantia Roll, marked on a small scroll above it as the 'Royal Banner'. Note the huge variety of pennant designs and the decoration of lances. This may be a composite unit with each rank made up from a different hussar troop that took part in the ceremonial entry. It was, however, quite normal for a proportion of men within a single troop to wear animal skins while others wore patterned capes. (Royal Castle, Warsaw)

11

An hussar formation, made up of several 'banners', prepares to charge into the Swedish lines at Kircholm (1605). In front is a group of unarmoured musicians, behind an officer with a mace. From the 'Battle of Kircholm' painting by an unknown artist of the early 17th century. (Château de Sassenage)

bands of peasants were particularly effective during the Swedish invasion of 1655–60; the Swedes were terrified of the deep Polish forests, where they were often ambushed by these scythe-wielding rustics.

The command of the armed forces of both Poland and Lithuania was ultimately in the hands of the king. He appointed for life the commanders of the army: the Grand Hetman of the Crown, the Field Hetman of the Crown, and similar posts in the Lithuanian army. The Field Hetman was only marginally inferior to the Grand Hetman, his main duty being to look after the standing army.

The Polish Autorament

The Polish army was organised along two fairly distinct models, and so can be divided into two sections: the 'Foreign *Autorament*' (contingent or 'enlistment') composed of troops raised along foreign lines, especially German; and the 'Polish *Autorament*', organised and dressed along more traditional and Eastern lines.

The organisation of the Polish Autorament was descended directly from the division of a mediaeval army into 'lances', 'banners', and 'battles'. In Poland *poczet* ('post'), *chorągiew* and *pulk* were the corresponding terms.

The smallest Polish unit was the 'post', derived from the mediaeval 'lance'. This comprised a *towarzysz* (comrade) and between one and 24 *pacholeks* (retainers or followers), depending on the rank and wealth of the comrade. In the hussars in the earlier period about four retainers per comrade was the average, reducing by the battle of Vienna to only two; in the 'cossacks' the number was always smaller, originally around three but reducing to one. The light cavalry in the later 17th century had only one retainer, and moves were made from above to take even this away. The 'post' of the *rotmistrz* ('rotamaster') was considerably bigger than those of his comrades; many of his 'horses', by which the unit's pay was calculated, were in fact 'dead-pays', which meant the *chorągiew* was usually between five and ten per cent smaller than its official strength.

In addition to these each 'post' had a number of camp servants, often including wives and other women, whose duties were to look after the wagons and provisions.

The smallest tactical unit of the Polish Contingent was the *chorągiew* (literally 'banner' or 'ensign', though for clarity sometimes translated here as 'troop' for cavalry, and 'company' for infantry). It was commonly known as a *rota*, though this term went out of use in the first half of the 17th century. Each *chorągiew* had at its head a *rotmistrz* (rotamaster), who was issued with a commission ('letter of array') to raise a fixed number of men under a single flag. He gathered together trusted comrades, who in turn brought with them their own 'lads'. He appointed from among the comrades his own *porucznik* (lieutenant) as his second-in-command, an ensign-bearer to carry the unit's flag and usually a handful of drummers or pipers. A *chorągiew* could vary hugely in size, though this was usually a figure stated on the rotamaster's initial commission. Round figures were the most usual: in the hussars normally 100, 120, 150 or 200; for lighter cavalry from 60 to 150, though kings and

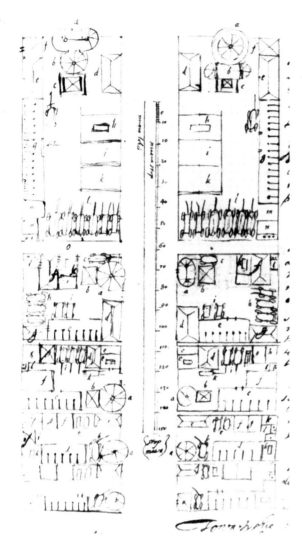

Layout of a camp for an hussar 'banner', c.1659. This has many interesting features, particularly the variation in the accommodation within the unit, from the huge quarters of the unit's two main officers, the rotamaster and lieutenant, down to the humbler ones of the junior 'comrades'. Each 'post' was a separate economic unit, with its own tents, wagons, stables, kitchen, bakery, and latrines, all of which are indicated on this drawing. Scale is in feet. From MS. of *Budownictwo Woiennego* ('Military Architecture') by Naronowicz-Naroński. (Warsaw Univ. Libr.)

hetmens' personal 'banners' were often larger.

Anything between two and 40 'banners' (more usually between five and 12) were grouped together into a *pulk*. The *pulk* was not a permanent organisation and had no staff aside from the senior rotamaster in the command, known as the *pulkownik*. The *pulk* was much like the feudal 'battle', though it had adapted somewhat to warfare in the 16th and 17th centuries. In many ways it was analagous to a modern army division or corps, containing a variety of troop types and able to fight independently of the main body of the army if necessary. It was only in the later part of the 17th century in the Foreign Contingent that the words *pulk* and *pulkownik* took on their modern meanings of regiment and colonel.

Cavalry

Until the middle of the 17th century Polish cavalry was divided into two main classes: hussars, and 'cossacks'. It was not until the late 1640s that a separate class of 'light cavalry' is mentioned in accounts and rolls; before this date such units went under the general heading of 'cossacks'.

The categories were fairly broad; the 'cossack', for instance, could have a wide variety of dress, weapons and armour. Some armoured cossack 'banners' were equipped at least as well as, if not better than, the poorer units of hussars. There are frequent references, for example, to armoured cossacks wearing hussar-style *szyszak* helmets, and hussars in *misiurka* mail helmets, so the distinction between the categories must occasionally have been fairly blurred. Later in the 17th century there are numerous examples of units being converted from armoured cossacks into hussars, and occasionally even vice versa.

During Bathory's Muscovite campaigns nearly a third of cavalry 'banners' were of mixed type, with a proportion of a different type of cavalry in the same *rota*: usually hussar units with an admixture of cossacks. In most units this usually only amounted to a few per cent of the total strength of the unit, though in a handful it reached half. By the 1590s such mixed units had disappeared.

Even within a homogenous unit there must have been great variation in dress worn by men of differing rank and wealth. Certainly hussar retainers would have been considerably less well equipped than their masters, and would have worn blackened armour and simple 'Pappenheimer' helmets, rather than the more elaborate items worn by 'comrades' and officers. In many instances they went entirely without armour—several accounts specifically mention that the retainers of the Polish Contingent were continually in danger of being mistaken for Tartars.

Hussars (*Husaria*)

The Polish hussar was certainly one of the most spectacular soldiers of all time. Contemporaries marvelled at them, and were frequently provoked into long-winded eulogies. For example the Frenchman Dupont, who served in Sobieski's artillery, thought that the hussars, 'by their fine appearance, the beauty of their arms and horses, and by the wealth of their equipment, surpass infinitely what writers tell us of the Persians, Greeks and Ancient Romans and everything that one can see in Europe and Asia.' Even the ever-critical Dalérac, the secretary to Sobieski's wife, remarked that the hussars were 'without a doubt, the most beautiful cavalry in Europe'.

Not all contemporaries were so easily impressed—one rather disgruntled Danziger in 1598 had quite a different opinion:

'I saw many Polish riders go by,
They had wings but couldn't fly.'
Not content with this he went on:
'The Poles carry long lances,
A short pennant thereon,
They might instead use a cowtail;
It costs not much and serves just as well.'

The hussar originated in Serbia towards the end of the 14th century. There are references to hussars in Poland in Treasury registers of 1500, though they were probably in Polish service before this date.

These early formations were foreign mercenaries, first known as *Racowie* from the term *Rascia*, 'Serbia', from the original centre of the Serbian state, Ras. The term 'hussar' probably originates not—as has been widely published—from any contrived connections with the Hungarian *husz* meaning 'twenty', but from *gussar*, a Slavonic word meaning 'bandit'. This gives us a fairly vivid idea of

The kapalin *helmet is a distinctive off-shoot of the standard* szyszak; *Bochenski, one of the foremost of Polish armour experts, dates this type to the last quarter of the 16th century, though pictures from as late as 1627 seem to show it still in use, and helmets of similar style were popular in the West during the Thirty Years' War. Note in particular the heart-shaped screw keeping the nose-guard in place, and the plume-holder at the rear. A whole wagon-load of* kapalin *helmets was recovered from the Vistula earlier this century. (MWP, 305*)*

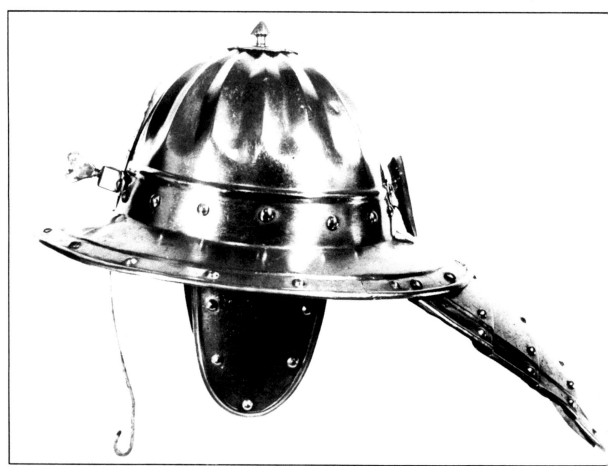

the nature of the early hussars—they were a light cavalry fighting in the style of bands of robbers. From surviving pictorial sources of the early hussars we can see that they were dressed in Hungarian fashion, frequently wearing the *magierka* (Hungarian cap), and at first no defensive armour. They fought in a supporting rôle for the cumbersome Western-style knights then predominant in Poland. As armoured knights were gradually phased out the hussars took their place, donning first ring-mail, helmets, and then plate armour.

The evolution of hussars in Poland and Hungary proceeded in parallel until the end of the 16th century. It was only in the 17th century that the Polish hussars began to differ significantly from the Hungarians, because the disastrous wars in Hungary prevented further development. While Polish hussars grew heavier, Hungarian hussars became lighter again; and it was from the latter that the hussar formations of the West developed. Even so, the typical dress of 19th-century hussars— braided fur-lined dolmans and pelisses, fur busbies with cloth bags, and close fitting trousers—are all features that can be traced to the basic dress worn by Polish hussars of the 16th and 17th centuries when not in full armour.

The many types of hussar armour are still difficult to date accurately. However, Bochenski has been able to classify such armour into several groups with similar characteristics, and date some items specifically in each group. It is usually possible to date most items to within about 30 years. (Of course, because an item is dated to an earlier period, this does not mean that it would not still have been worn later on—though among the more fashionable elements of the nobility, who changed their appearance almost as frequently as today, this might not have been true.)

The 'wings' of the Polish hussars, perhaps their most characteristic feature, seem to be closely linked with their origins in Serbia, and were certainly in use outside Poland, though they did not develop into such elaborate forms. The *delis* or 'hot-heads' of the Turkish army, famous for their display of wings and feathers in the most bizarre of fashions, were in fact mainly Serbians and not Turks at all; there is even a good deal of evidence to suggest that *delis* served in the Polish army as well.

The function of the wings has been (and will

Polish hussar on a woodcut titled *Wizerunek Zolnierza Polskiego* ('Likeness of a Polish Soldier') from the book *Pobudka zacnym synom Korony Polskiej do Sluzby Wojennej . . .* ('Call to arms of worthy sons of the Polish Crown to Military Service . . .'), by **Wojciech Rakowski, 1620: a forerunner of the modern recruiting poster.**

probably always be) a source of speculation and curiosity. Theories have included their being a defence against sword-cuts, or against lassoes; a souvenir worn only by veterans of wars against the Turks; or an attempt to make the wearers look like angels! Aside from the obvious motive, of simply wanting to look splendid, by far the most likely answer now appears to be that they were used as a device for scaring the enemy, especially the enemy's horses—not by any whistling sounds that they are alleged to have made, but by sheer visual impact. The wearing of wings is linked so closely with the wearing of furs that it would seem that the furs, wings and fluttering pennants were, in fact, all part of the same device.

Raising hussars was exorbitantly expensive, most of the cost being due to the extraordinary cost of the horses, often worth between five and ten times the annual salary of an hussar. Polish horses were unquestionably among the finest in Europe, and laws were passed to prevent their export, as their military value was fully appreciated.

It is still difficult to say exactly what hussars wore in the field. Certainly, in civilian life, hussars—who came from the most fashionable and peacockish sections of society—would not begrudge spending vast fortunes on their dress and equipment. As Grammont mentions in 1664: 'There is such rivalry among them, that they all try to surpass each other in the beauty of their arms'. There was consequently very little uniformity in a hussar unit: men wore whatever colours they liked, and dressed as splendidly as they could afford.

The main weapon of the hussars was the lance, used in conjunction with two swords: a sabre (*szabla*) worn from a waist belt on the left side, and a long sword, either a *pallasz* or a *koncerz*, carried on the horse, usually under the left side of the saddle. The importance of firearms among the hussars has been much underestimated—they were required to carry a pair of pistols in saddle holsters certainly as early as 1576, and they occasionally carried carbines as well.

In Bathory's day hussars were by far the most numerous type of cavalry, representing about 85 per cent of all the army's cavalry. The proportion gradually decreased, so that in the second half of the 17th century they numbered variously between 1,000 and 4,000 horses or between five and 20 per cent of the cavalry.

Most hussar units were commanded by high state dignitaries; voivodes, officers of the crown, hetmen, even bishops had their own 'banners'. Such units were rarely commanded in person by these dignitaries, their functions being delegated to lieutenants.

Though hussar 'banners' invariably took their titles from their commanders' name, and so changed with every change of commander, many units had traditions stretching back over many decades. At Vienna, for instance, Prince Jacob's 'banner' had previously belonged to King Michael Wiśniowiecki, and before that to King John Casimir. Sobieski's Royal 'banner' had previously been commanded by Jerzy Lubomirski, famed in the wars against Sweden and Muscovy, and in the Lubomirski Rebellion.

Each 'banner' had its own pennant design and colours. At Vienna the colours of the most famous units were as follows:

Sobieski	. . .	Crimson and blue
Prince Jacob	. . .	Yellow and red
Prince Alexander	. . .	Black and yellow
Grand Marshal,		
Lubomirski	. . .	Red and white
Voivode of Cracow,		
Potocki	. . .	Black and yellow

Hussar armour, c.1630, recovered together with a mail shirt from the grave of King Vladislav's secretary Stanislaw Skórkowski. The suit is of the 'older' type, and consists of breast and backplates, gorget, shoulder- and arm-guards, and helmet all in matching style with decoration in brass. The helmet has a simple hemispherical skull. Note the openwork heart on the helmet's ear flap—heart emblems are typical for Polish hussars, and also occur on Polish Highlanders' brooches. (MWP, 678*)

Pancerni Cossacks

'Cossacks' were much cheaper to raise than hussars. They made up in the 1580s barely ten per cent of the cavalry, but by the 1680s this had increased to over 60 per cent.

For most of the period 'cossacks' were in fact raised from all corners of Poland, and shared only their name with the true or Zaporozhian Cossacks. The name does, however, originate from the Cossack peoples, and the earliest units were no doubt raised from true Cossacks.

In Lithuania this type of cavalry was known by the name of a Circassian people, the '*Petyhorcy*' from the region of the 'Five Hills' (Piaty Hory) in the Caucasus. Starowolski in the 1620s also mentions a type of mail-armoured cavalry in use in Poland called '*Czemerysy*'. These are something of a mystery still, though they are undoubtedly connected with a steppe people of this name; Dalérac identifies them with Tartars settled in the Polish Ukraine. In any event it is certain that this type of cavalry, particularly when clad in mail, owed a great deal to the steppe peoples living in the south-eastern regions of the Republic and beyond.

During the rebellions of the true (that is Zaporozhian) Cossacks from 1648 onward, in order to distinguish Polish 'cossack' formations from the rebels, their name was rather tactfully altered to *pancerni* 'cossacks' or simply *pancerni* (literally 'mail-coated men').

The cossacks were always an extremely mobile arm mounted on light, but fast and enduring horses. Many units were completely unarmoured, though even the armoured variety could perform all the functions expected of light cavalry. They combined the elusiveness of the Tartars with the ability to provide concentrated fire on a given point in the enemy line in the manner of the Western 'caracole'. As well as providing flank cover and preparing the way for carefully co-ordinated assaults by the hussars, they could provide a useful charging cavalry, especially when armed with lances.

Breastplate ornaments on hussar armour were made of brass, and followed a small number of patterns. The so-called 'Knight's Cross' was the most common. Plaques bearing the Virgin Mary were probably related to the 'Order of the Immaculate Conception' which King Vladislav tried to initiate in 1634, but which failed because of opposition from the Seym. He did, however, succeed in forming a brotherhood connected with the order, to which many nobles in the hussars belonged; and it seems that many hussars wore such plaques until the brotherhood's disbandment in about 1674, a date which ties in well with the dating of hussar armour by other methods. From Skórkowski's armour, *c*.1630. (MWP, 678*)

The Lisowski Cossacks

The founder of this famous band of volunteers was Aleksander Lisowski, 'a rebel and general no-gooder' as the Lithuanian Field Hetman Chodkiewicz called him. He actually died in 1616 before his cossacks had got up to most of their mischief, but in tribute to their old commander the name was kept on. They fought as an unofficial army for the King of Poland, receiving no wages for their services, but being more than recompensed by a free

An unusual suit of mixed mail and scale, in the 'Sarmatian' style, perhaps designed for a *pancerni* officer. Late 17th or early 18th century. (Kórnik Castle)

hand in the gathering of booty. They served on secret missions to destabilise border areas of Muscovy, and so were one of the main cutting edges of Poland in the Muscovite 'Time of Troubles'. Their part in the Thirty Years' War, as clandestine aid from the King of Poland to the Holy Roman Emperor, brought them into the West, where they fought in Germany, Hungary, Italy, France and Holland. In an age of barbarous warfare they were singled out by Western commentators as something special, earning an impressive reputation for pillaging and general brigandry, which did not stop when they returned to Poland. Attempts were made to stamp out this plague of robbery every time the Lisowczyks came home: they were declared outlaws, and were executed without mercy when caught.

Lisowczyks were mainly made up of the cavalry known in Poland as 'cossacks', and composed initially of various Eastern peoples aside from Poles: Lithuanians, Tartars, Zaporozhian and even Don Cossacks. However, in Imperial service the bulk were Poles. As unpaid volunteers the Lisowczyks were less uniformly and more poorly equipped than the regular army. They were nicknamed (we hear from Debolecki, their chaplain) 'Leopold's flowers', after their variety of colourful dress. In Western service they must have picked up a great deal of Western equipment, for we hear that when they returned to Poland they were examined with a great deal of curiosity. They received standards from the Emperor, which were probably in the usual Imperial style. They were organised into 'banners', which all belonged to a single *pulk* ('battle'), commanded by a *pulkownik* democratically elected from among the rotamasters. The *pulkownik* also had command over two 'banners' known as the Red and Black Rotas, though it is not clear exactly how these colour designations applied.

Light Cavalry

Initially these were provided by light-armed cossack and Tartar units raised within Poland; however, as cossacks became steadily heavier, increasing use was made of unarmoured cavalry raised abroad—particularly in Wallachia. In the last half of the 17th century the light cavalry was made up of units designated either 'Wallachian' or 'Tartar', though this was little more than

Hussar and '*pancerni*' cossack in 1693, both armed with lances. The hussar has several remarkable features: the armour cuisses (thigh guards), the 'Gorgon' plaque worn on the shoulder, and the quartered lance pennant—this pattern appears most frequently on late 17th-century Polish battle paintings, though it is more commonly two-tailed. It is interesting to note that the fanciful baroque representations of 17th-century soldiers actually began to influence the 'Sarmatian' style of armour worn in Poland. From an allegory to the triumph of Sobieski in a book by Jakub Kazimierz Haur. (National Library, Warsaw)

reference to their mode of dress and equipment, since a substantial proportion of the men were Poles who could not afford to enlist as *pancerni*. Many light cavalry units were mixed, containing a proportion of men equipped in each style. By the Vienna campaign these units were titled simply 'light cavalry' with no distinction between types, and numbered about 15 per cent of the cavalry. (Wallachians and Tartars will be dealt with in more detail in Part 2.)

Infantry

The native infantry were not at first very highly valued, and came a very poor second after the cavalry; the nobility generally regarded them with contempt. Starowolski, for example, wrote: 'We use them not so much for fighting but as labourers, building ramparts, digging ditches, erecting bridges, clearing roads for the guns and heavier

Attachments for a pair of wings to the backplate of hussar armour. The wings, made from a line of feathers inserted into a brass-edged wooden frame, were mounted on brackets or hinges. The design of these brackets varied but they usually kept the wing rigidly in place. (MWP)

of the fact that nobles, in the tradition of mediaeval chivalry still prevalent in 17th-century Poland, regarded war as the domain of the nobility, and a sport that peasants were simply not fit to join in. Attempts were made to recruit units of infantry from the nobility, but this proved unpopular, and was discontinued. Yet the raw material for a solid infantry arm was in fact there all the time: it was simply the training that had been lacking. Foreigners were most impressed by the infantry later in the century. Ogier, a French diplomat, noted of them in 1635: 'Nowhere for certain in the world can you find people of more vigorous and strong appearance; they scare you just by their faces and manner of walking. Besides they all have heads marked by the Muscovites and Turks with terrible scars, and since their heads are shaved, these wounds are visible'.

Early Polish Infantry

The early Polish infantry was raised in a similar manner to the cavalry: the rotamaster selected 'comrades' who brought with them their followers. Units were raised of between 150 and 200 men. The unit was divided into tens, with *dziesiętniks* ('tenth-men') in command of each file. Pikeman or pavise-bearers stood in the front rank or two; behind them, men armed mainly with firearms. One flag was carried for approximately every 50 men in the unit, and the *rota* was often equipped with a few horses.

A roll of the *rota*, under Kasper Stuzinski, rotamaster of the castle of Kiev, 'for 200 *draby* (infantrymen)' dated October 1577, is one of the last records of the old Polish type of infantry, which had by this date mainly been replaced by *haiduks*. It contained 34 pikemen (*kopijniks*) and 111 arquebusiers, two drummers, and six flags. Each 'ten' was in fact of only seven or eight men, of which two were armed with pikeman's plate armour, helmet (*przylbica*), pike, and sword; the remainder had firearms, swords, and occasionally helmets as well. The 'pikemen' are unlikely to have fought in separate pike blocks; rather, they were immediate protection for the unarmoured arquebusiers. The *rota* also included four mounted men in mailshirts with *rohatyna* lances and bows[1].

wagons. If we desire to capture a town we hire Germans or Hungarians, who are much better trained than our men'.

Whether the nobility were simply afraid of arming the peasantry, from whom most of the infantry were recruited, is another consideration. Of course, the huge distances that such troops would have to cover on foot in Poland made it more efficient to concentrate on the cavalry arm rather than the infantry. We must, however, take account

[1]AGAD: Ask 85, 62

Haiduks

Haiduk derives from the Turkish *haidud* meaning 'marauder'. Haiduks came to Poland by way of Hungary, and were very quickly adopted as the standard model for Polish infantry. The best haiduks were raised from the Carpathian Mountains and states to the south of Poland. Contemporaries frequently remark on the large stature of haiduks, 'huge of body like giants', and on their reputation for rough living and general ferocity.

Polish haiduks were organised into *rotas* as in the old Polish infantry, but not raised along lines of the 'comrade' system. A *rota* numbered usually between 100 and 200 men, divided into 'tens' as before, but now without any form of armour or helmets in the ranks. Haiduks were armed almost exclusively with firearms alone; 'tenth-men' now carried the *darda*, a staff weapon. (This seems to have been used mainly to assist with fire control rather than for combat.) On occasion 'tenth-men' were also issued with firearms.

It may seem strange that an army so full of cavalry rarely used the pike—even Western mercenaries in Polish service were usually equipped with firearms alone. The reason for this was that the rôle of infantry was strictly defined as fire support for the cavalry strike force, or for defending or attacking obstacles. They were rarely called upon to fight hand-to-hand in the open field. Their vulnerability to attack by cavalry was countered by the Polish cavalry, whose usual immense superiority over the enemy cavalry allowed them also to act as a shield for the infantry. However, haiduks were quite able to hold their own in combat with Western pike-

Most hussar lances seem to have followed the same basic design throughout the period. They were usually about five metres long, made from two separate pieces hollowed out for lightness, and decoratively painted or covered in a pattern uniform for the entire troop. The handgrip, of polygonal section, had above it a flattened ball hand-guard. Note in particular the painted-on feathers. (PAN Library, Kórnik)

and-shot formations, as they demonstrated on several occasions—the most notable being the battle of Lubieszów (1577), where Bathory's haiduk guard was largely responsible for the rout of six large mercenary German *knecht* companies.

After the Swedish Wars of the late 1620s it is clear that contact with Gustavus's much-improved infantry, in several incidents where the Poles came off worse, led to a recognition of the value of mixed pike/shot formations; and measures were taken to reorganise the Polish infantry along Western lines. So began the decline of the haiduk; and by 1665 Cefali was able to say that haiduks had mostly fallen out of use. By Sobieski's reign only a handful of units remained in the service of the king, hetmen, and the wealthier magnates, as ceremonial or bodyguard companies. By the 18th century haiduks had degenerated into little more than noblemen's table-servants and doormen.

Wybraniecka infantry

This translates as 'draughted' infantry rather than the more literal 'selected', which has overtones of excellence: an élite formation this most definitely was not. The *Wybraniecka* infantry were established on the basis of an act of the Seym and a decree issued by King Bathory in 1578, on the pattern of similar peasant levies in his Transylvanian home. One peasant infantryman with full equipment and uniform was to be raised for each 20 Polish acres (*lan*) of all royal estates. The uniform, which was to be provided by the men themselves, was in the standard Hungarian haiduk pattern and no different from that of the regulars, in the standard colour of 'cloudy' blue.

Bathory had hoped to raise 15,000 men by this conscription, but the lack of commitment from reluctant farmers and village officials meant that the most he ever got was about 2,000. These men did play a useful part in Bathory's Muscovite campaigns, even carrying out several moderately successful storming operations; but it was clear from the start that they were unwilling fighters. Plagued by an appalling desertion rate, they were increasingly given fewer combat duties. An instruction issued by King Vladislav in 1633 gave specific instructions for them to be equipped with entrenching tools, and not to bother at all with firearms or uniform: this leaves little doubt as to how highly they were valued. They were still being raised during the Vienna campaign, but were now distributed among the regular units rather than in separate units.

The Lithuanian Army

The Lithuanian army differed little in its dress and organisation from the Polish. It was commanded by its own Grand Hetman and Field Hetman, who occasionally took command of the Crown army—as did Lithuanian Field Hetman Jan Karol Chodkiewicz at Chocim in 1621.

According to the *Komput* the Lithuanian army was between a third and half the size of the Polish one; when plans were made to raise a Crown army

Pennants occurred in various designs throughout the period, and were either single or double-tailed and made of silk. Length seems to have varied from about 1.5 to 4 metres. They were invariably (except perhaps in the Royal Troop) uniform for the whole troop.

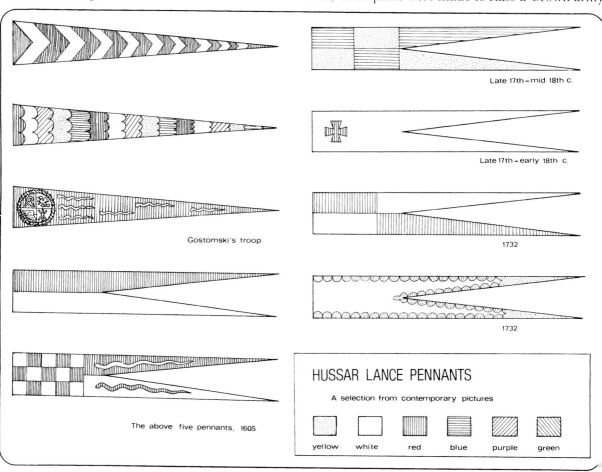

Gostomski's troop

The above five pennants, 1605

Late 17th–mid 18th c.

Late 17th–early 18th c.

1732

1732

HUSSAR LANCE PENNANTS

A selection from contemporary pictures

yellow   white   red   blue   purple   green

of 36,000 men, as at Vienna, the Lithuanians were usually called upon for only 12,000.

The only major difference in the Lithuanian army was that *pancerni* or armoured 'cossacks' were known instead as *Petyhorcy*. Their equipment was slightly different, too; they were armed with *rohatyna* lances rather than the firearms normal for the Polish *pancerni* before 1676. It is quite probable that these units were more markedly Eastern in appearance than the Poles.

In many ways the Lithuanian army was more Polish than the Polish army. The Foreign Contingent in it was always considerably smaller; and while the Polish generals and nobles talked in a mixture of Latin and Polish, and occasionally dressed in Western fashion, the Lithuanian nobility cultivated the Polish language and traditions to distinguish themselves from their own peasantry, who spoke mainly Ruthenian.

The Lithuanians were, if anything, even wilder than the Poles. They were renowned for their looting, largely due to the fact that they often went without pay for years at a time. During the Vienna campaign Dalérac noted that 'the Lithuanians have such a bad reputation for pillage and disorder on the march, that the Imperial Commissaries begged the King of Poland to divert this plague away from their country, and to have their army pass through by the Mountains of Hungary'.

The Lithuanian army contained a large proportion of Tartars, and so their tactics were based on the use of fewer rigid formations of troops. The pictures made by the Swede, Dahlberg, during the Swedish invasion of Poland in 1655–60 show the Lithuanian army drawn up in a huge circular fan, with apparently no solid formations. Though this is no doubt an exaggeration, other battle accounts do seem to suggest that the Lithuanians fought in very much looser and less formal formations than the Poles, particularly in later years.

There was a great deal of rivalry and distrust between the Poles and Lithuanians; Pasek, for example, calls the Lithuanians 'beet-eaters' in a slighting reference to their staple diet.

Hussar lance pennant, probably from 1680–1775, though this pattern is likely to have been used earlier. It is made from silk, one half crimson, the other white. The Knight's Cross is sewn in reverse colours. Length 390 cm, width 79 cm, distance to fork 104 cm. There are nine original hussar pennants in the Polish Army Museum, two of this pattern, seven of the pattern on Plate F. (MWP, 665*)

Pospolite Ruszenie (Levy of the Nobility)

The mobilisation of the nobility *en masse* to fight an external threat was a relic of feudalism. It survived in Poland, however, throughout the 17th century, though it was by this time a completely out-dated institution.

There were two levels of Levy; the 'Small', for quelling localised disturbances, and the 'Grand', for situations that threatened the very existence of the state, and for which the king had to be personally in command. The state could reputedly assemble by this method forces of well over 100,000 men—though modern estimates, e.g. by Wimmer, put the Grand Levy of the Crown at closer to 40,000.

The Levy was organised into provincial units according to palatinate (*województwo*), land (*ziemia*) and district (*powiat*). The levy of each region was commanded by a high civil dignitary, usually the castellan, who assumed the rank of *pulkownik* of the forces of his district. The nobility of the district were

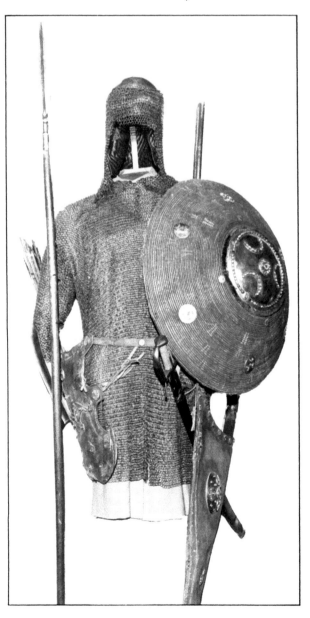

divided up into 'banners' of horse and foot, organised in the Polish manner; and commanded by a rotamaster, often a retired professional soldier appointed from the district's nobility. The exact ratio of foot to horse varied depending on the particular speciality of the district, the poorer nobility of, e.g., Mazowsze providing more infantry than a relative wealthy region such as Sandomierz. There was normally a preponderence of 'cossack'-type units, these being the easiest to form with the resources available to the average nobleman. The nobility of each province were required to turn up for annual reviews, where in theory their equipment was checked and they were given training. In practice these events inevitably became little more than social and political get-togethers, with the real business being conveniently relegated to a minor rôle.

The fighting value of the Levy was rarely very high, particularly in the more peaceful western provinces of Poland, Wielkopolska and Malopolska. The Levies of Lithuania and Polish Russia were, however, of much higher quality—the regular Tartar raids had shaped them into a solid fighting force that could be assembled quickly and to great effect.

The Levy suffered from appalling indiscipline: the proud and argumentative Polish noblemen were hard to command at the best of times, but gathered together in thousands they became almost totally unmanageable. They grumbled, questioned orders, and swore openly at officers, including the king. Assembling the Levy in one place was a feat in itself, and an operation that took several months. Once together the party began in earnest, with each noble bringing all his home comforts, all the food he would need, and an ample supply of alcohol.

Keeping the Levy together was another problem panic broke out easily, and men were liable to ride

Equipment of a *pancerni* cavalryman, second half of the 17th century. The Oriental appearance of the armour is most striking. Much of it was taken as war booty on campaigns in the East, though most of it was produced in Polish workshops. The *kalkan* round shield made of fig wood is of Turkish origin. The mail coat is made of fairly large rings, so allowing the colour of the undergarments to show through. However, this image of the *pancerni* is probably much overstylised by modern authorities, and on campaign men would have had a very much less Eastern appearance. The chief armament for much of the 17th century was the wheellock carbine, and as many pistols as could be comfortably tucked away on rider and horse. (MWP, photo: Miroslaw Ciunowicz)

Siege of Pskov, 1581:
1: Lithuanian infantryman
2: Hussar 'Comrade', 1560–1590
3: Hungarian Haiduk officer, 1577
4: Hungarian Haiduk infantryman, 1577

A

Entry of Queen Constantia, Cracow, 1605:
1: Rotamaster of Hussars   **2: Hussar 'Comrade'**

B

Polish Haiduks, 1600-1625:
1: Haiduk Arquebusier
2: 'Tenth-man', Gostomski's Company, 1605

3: Bagpiper, Stradom Town Guard, 1605
4: Rotamaster
5: Rotamaster's Boy

C

1: Light-armed cavalryman, 1600-1625
2: Polish 'Cossack' cavalry officer, 1600-1625
3,4: Peasant infantrymen, 1630s

D

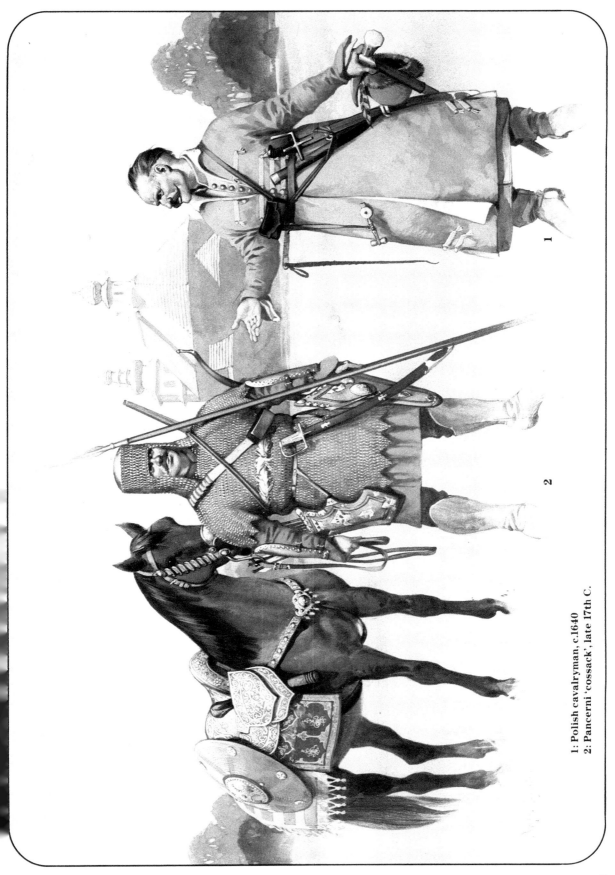

1: Polish cavalryman, c.1640
2: Pancerni 'cossack', late 17th C.

E

Polish Hussar 'Comrade', 1672-83

1

Moldavian, Wallachian & Hungarian
campaigns, 1685-91:
1: Grand Hetman Stanislaw Jablonowski, 1682-1702
2: Bunczuk-Bearer

1

2

G

1: Banner of District of Grodno, Lithuania
2: Banner of the Court Army of King Sigismund III, 1621

3: Standard of 'Cossack' troop led by Jan Slawinski,
   Sword-Bearer of Starodub, Lithuania
4: Standard of Hetman or Grand Marshal, first half 17th C.

off for home at the first hint of danger. The worst example occurred at Pilawice in 1648, during the Cossack wars, when rumours that a Tartar force was coming to assist the Cossacks caused the entire army to disintegrate overnight. As Hauteville noted in his *Account of Poland*:

'The disorder was so great and the flight so precipitate, that the Cossacks were for a whole day of opinion, that it was only a feint to draw them from their post; but at last having detached some troops to observe the Enemy, they understood that their was not one soldier in the Polish camp.'

Although it was difficult to get the Levy to take offensive action, they were generally quite effective in defence, where the constant practice with the sword—carried by every nobleman as part of his dress—could be of real value. They were, however, a 'one-shot weapon', and would depart for home once their supplies had run out, or after taking part in a single battle, feeling their obligations fulfilled whether it had been a victory or defeat. It is small wonder that contemporaries were bitingly sarcastic about the Levy, and advised that the institution be abolished entirely. The old veteran Pasek grumbled, 'I would rather pasture pigs than command the Levy in attack'.

Flags, Command Insignia and Field Signs

Flags

Flags in the part of the army raised along Polish lines still displayed many clearly mediaeval features. Polish heavy cavalry carried large standards long after they had been replaced in the West, for reasons of convenience, by smaller ones. In Poland the logic still ran that the larger the standard the more important the status of the unit carrying it. The number of 'tails' on the flag was also related to the importance of the flag: flags of the various *powiaty* (districts), at least in Lithuania, were 'single-tailed'; those of palatinates were two-tailed, while those of the State or Court were usually three- or occasionally four-tailed. There are signs, however, that the Polish Contingent began to opt for smaller Western-style flags by the middle of the 17th century.

The commonest symbol on Polish flags was the national emblem: a silver or white eagle on a red field. Frequently the eagle was replaced by a simple white cross. The eagle and the cross had been in use as national emblems for many centuries, the cross already appearing on shields in the time of Mieszko I (*c*.963–992). It is likely that the ubiquitous white 'Knight's Cross' was simply a variant of the plain cross, and was worn as a national emblem. Lithuania used the *Pogoń* or 'Pursuit' emblem; a knight with raised sword on a charging horse in

The *misiurka* or Eastern mail-helmet consisted of a metal disc to which was attached a mail curtain. The disc usually had a hook in the centre from which the helmet could be hung when not in use, either from the waist belt, the saddle, or in the soldier's home. It is usually forgotten that some form of padded headwear would have been worn underneath to absorb blows inflicted on the helmet: such padding makes the helmet sit much higher on the head than might be expected.

proper colours, bearing on his shield the white 'Gończa' double cross.

The heraldic badge of the troop commander was also a very common device. Poland used a very simple heraldic system based on a relatively small number of clan badges, or *herby*. These were generally of simple design, most being combinations of arrow and horseshoe shapes; their origins are still largely mysterious. In the 13th and 14th centuries members of the same clan (and therefore heraldic badge) often fought together in the same battle units. However, by the battle of Grunwald (Tannenberg) in 1410, there were only two such clan units out of 50 'banners' taking part in the battle; and by the 16th century such military connections between bearers of the same clan badge had altogether vanished.

Figures of religious patrons were also commonly used on flags, particularly since most wars were at least partly motivated by religion. The Virgin Mary with Child, standing on a crescent moon with a sunburst background, was particularly favoured in Poland. Figures of various saints and angels, common particularly in the earlier period, were usually connected with local preferences in the area of recruitment.

Infantry colours in the Polish Autorament usually followed Imperial or Hungarian practices. Earlier in the period, colours were huge, thin silk flags, often over three metres in the fly. Devices were usually broad horizontal or vertical bands in differing colours, or crosses—the St. Andrew's Cross or St. George's Cross stretching across the entire field. The Burgundian *Raguly* or 'ragged' cross was also used, in reference to the Vasa kings' membership of the Hapsburgs' Catholic Order of the Golden Fleece.

Pancerni **'cossack', last quarter of the 17th century, from a 19th-century copy by Lesser of a lost painting by Polish court painter Jerzy Szymonowicz-Siemiginowski (died 1711). Note the pistol holster, the method of fastening the mail helmet, the jagged tooth cut of the mail shirt, and the** *dzida* **(short lance). (MWP)**

Insignia of Command

To identify their position in battle, hetmen carried special insignia. Hetman Jan Tarnowski in his *Consilium Rationis Bellicae* (1548) recommends that 'An insignium (*znak*) on a lance is to be carried beside the hetman, and not by any other'. At the end of the 16th century these insignia were simply personal flags carried on hussar-style lances, with a Hungarian cap attached at the lance head. Piotrowski, Bathory's secretary, describes a hetman's insignium used in the Pskov campaign of 1581, which had a red Hungarian cap with plume on the head of a lance, and below this a pennon with the inscription '*Fortitudo et Laus Mea Dominus*'.

Gradually, under Turkish influence, a very stylised insignium evolved: the *bunczuk*. The basic form of this is shown on Plate G2, though the exact design varied considerably, decoration usually being a combination of winglets made from real ostrich or crane feathers, horse-tails dyed in bright colours, and coloured ribbons of silk or linen. Only two original *bunczuks* survive, though there are many descriptions, and depictions on contemporary paintings.

The other chief distinguishing marks of command were maces and batons. The *bulawa* mace was the symbol of the hetman. Ceremonial models were usually spherical, onion- or pear-shaped, the surface being gilded or silvered, and encrusted with stones and jewels. Models for use in the field were somewhat less ornate. It became common by the 18th century to refer to the hetman's office itself as the *bulawa*.

The *buzdygan* mace was usually reserved for rotamasters. It was usually 'feathered', the head consisting of six or seven vanes arranged symmetrically around a central shaft. The shape of each vane varied; some were triangular, some leaf-like, some 's'-shaped, others even 'eagle-shaped'.

By the end of the period maces were falling out of combat use; Dalérac mentions that they were no longer used during the Vienna campaign, appear-

ing only in portraits and commemorative battle paintings. But not all the evidence supports his view. Rubinkowski in his *Janina* (1739) describes a curious party-piece that Sobieski apparently performed before the Allied commanders at Vienna. After mounting his horse he threw his *bulawa* into the air with his left hand, then quickly wheeled round and caught it in his right hand—'this in the presence of the Holy Roman Emperor, all the princes, generals and other officers, much to their amusement'.

Field signs

Field signs were vital to distinguish Poles in battle against enemies who were often dressed very

Fragment of a 'letter of nobility' awarded to Bernard Krzysztof Bernatowicz in 1676, showing a *pancerni* 'cossack' armed with an odd-looking lance decorated with striped pattern. This is perhaps either the *rohatyna* or *dzida* reintroduced into the Crown *pancerni* at approximately this time. It is interesting to note that the army was almost the only means of social advancement in Poland, the *pancerni* providing the easiest prospects—perhaps this is a portrait? (AGAD, perg 6154, Warsaw)

Koniuszny (**Equerry**) **Gamocki (equerry was a civil title), wearing typical equipment of a** *pancerni* **officer, during the tournament held in Sweden to honour the accession of Karl XI in 1672. Gamocki was one of the few Poles taking part in this event, the other 'Poles' being dressed-up Swedes. After a print in** *Certamen Equestre,* **usually credited to Georg Christoph Eimmart. (MWP)**

similarly, particularly the Turks, Cossacks and Tartars. At Vienna many authorities note that twists of straw were worn to identify the Poles. Later on, in the Wallachian campaigns, Dalérac mentions that the Poles tied white handkerchiefs around their left arms so that newly arrived troops from Brandenburg could tell the Poles from the Tartars.

In the occasional civil wars there was often confusion because the antagonists wore identical clothes. At the battle of Mątwy (1666), during the disastrous Lubomirski Rebellion, the rebels were wearing a kerchief tied on the left arm, but Pasek mentions that even these were of little value: 'We rode into each other's midst, knowing not who was who; before attacking anyone you first asked: "Whose army are you in?" "Whose are you in?" If the adversary's then: "Let's fight!" "Go to the Devil!"'

The Poles frequently sang religious songs to stir up their courage: again, a passage from Pasek just before crossing the Polish border *en route* for Denmark in 1658: 'The whole army began to sing *O*

Gloriosa Domina! in the Polish way. While the horses in all the regiments snorted so ferociously that our spirits rose . . .' Odlanicki describes a battle against the Muscovites in 1660: 'The order was given for us to attack in the name of the Lord, accompanied by the playing of various military music, singing *O Gloriosa!*, calling Our Lady for assistance, with our hearts high, after the chaplain's benediction, we advanced . . .'

The Plates

A: Siege of Pskov, 1581
The Muscovite campaigns of Stefan Bathory (1579–82) were hindered by the bitter Russian weather. This scene is based on contemporary remarks that soldiers often froze to death, even on horseback. The Englishman Mundy, for example, saw: 'Horses' noses and men's beards hang dangling with icicles', and heard of: 'countrymen coming on sleds . . . frozen stiff stark dead, still holding the bridle or reins in their hands, standing or sitting as alive guiding their horses. Others have been brought in so on horseback, their stiff benumbed limbs keeping them fast in the saddle. A soldier standing sentinel with his musket on his rest hath been found in that posture, stark dead and stiff with cold. These are common reports'.

A1: Lithuanian infantryman
The Lithuanians at first had much in common with their Muscovite neighbours. They wore Muscovite-style long, padded kaftans with high collars, essential in the Lithuanian winters, which were matched in severity only by those of Muscovy. The quilting gave protection not only against the cold but also as a form of armour. King Bathory showed interest in such kaftans; in a letter of 1577 to the Livonian hetman he wrote: 'It was brought to our attention, that Your Honour, has had a silk kaftan made, which is proof even against bullets. We instruct Your Honour to send it to us most urgently with the craftsmen who made it . . .' Lithuanians seem to have abandoned their Muscovite tendencies in fashion by the beginning of the 17th century and were afterwards dressed in similar manner to the Poles.

The figure here is based on Lithuanians in engravings by Adelhauser & Zündt (1567) and Vecellio (1590s). According to Vecellio, Lithuanians wore red hats lined in a different colour. His arquebus bag is reconstructed from early 17th-century Hungarian and Polish prints. Such bags were probably used by most soldiers (see also C1).

A2: Hussar 'Comrade', 1560–90

King Bathory brought with him several 'banners' of Hungarian hussars as part of his Guard when he arrived in Poland in 1576. Hussars were, however, already the predominant type of cavalry in Poland. The use of white and black bearskins is mentioned, for example in Orzelski's account of Bathory's entry into Cracow in 1576. The figure is based mainly on a woodcut in a book by Czahrowski (1598), and on hussars in De Bruyn's book of 1575 *Diversum gentium armatura equestris*. The gilded *szyszak* helmet is of the Hungarian style worn by wealthier hussars in the 16th century (MWP). Wings worn tacked onto curved wing-shape shields were the forerunners of the more stylised wing-shaped ornaments. Shields were carried by hussars until the 1570s, though many accounts speak of them still being in use well into the '80s and '90s.

A3: Hungarian Haiduk Officer, 1577

Bathory's Hungarian and Transylvanian haiduk guard came to Poland with him in 1576. They differed little in dress from the Poles, though because of the warmer Hungarian climate their clothes tended to be somewhat less substantial, and usually shorter in cut. This officer has an overgarment shorter than his undergarment, whereas the Pole's would usually be of equal length. Generally speaking the infantryman's dress was hopelessly inadequate: during the Pskov campaign, Piotrowski notes after the first snows: 'Fur-coats begin to fetch a good price . . . but with the poor infantryman in the earthworks, God only knows what will happen'.

The figure is based on Abraham de Bruyn's costume book of 1581. The dangerous-looking spiked *buzdygan* mace was once in the collection of Jan Strzalecki; it is very similar to the one being carried in de Bruyn's engraving. The sword is a Hungarian '*Batorówka*'-type sabre, with characteristic long quillons, named after King Bathory because of the picture of the king on the blade (MWP). Gloves are restored from an officer in the '*Pattern of Costumes*' painting.

'Death and the nobleman', a stucco relief in Tarlów parish church, dated to shortly after 1640: perhaps the clearest existing illustration of the dress and equipment of an unarmoured Polish cavalryman. He wears typical Polish dress: *zupan* undergarment, *kontusz* overcoat, fur-lined *kuczma* cap with feather, and high leather boots. The whip, cap, haircut and lack of spurs are typical Tartar features copied widely in Poland. Note in particular the winder key for a wheellock firearm hanging from an ammunition pouch. (Polish Institute of Art, Warsaw)

A4: Hungarian Haiduk, 1577

Based on de Bruyn's costume book *Omnium poene gentium imagines . . .* (1577). He wears the very characteristic pillbox-shaped *magierka* (Hungarian cap), with peak and side flaps folded down in the cold weather. These caps were usually made of felt or thick cloth in various designs; they were commonly black, though many other colours were used. His simple sleeveless cape is a type seen in pictures of Poles and Hungarians throughout the period and widely worn throughout the army. The jacket has the curious split skirt joined by braiding which seems to have been fashionable in the 1570s. His sword is the typical open-hilted Hungarian sabre carried widely in both Hungary and Poland.

Bathory's footguard is described by Orzelski in 1576 during Bathory's arrival in Cracow as 'composed of Haiduks, Hungarians, Poles, and Circassians. They had long firearms, curved sabres, axes that were easy to throw; the age of all was young, their stature enormous; they were dressed in a violet colour'. Bathory's Hungarian haiduks differed slightly from Polish haiduks in that they were formed into regiments of between 500 and 3,000 men, which in turn were divided into *rotas* of 100 men; Polish haiduks do not appear to have used such large permanent groupings. These men earned a fearful reputation in Poland, for both their efficiency and their cruelty, especially among Polish nobility—who were frightened that Bathory

would use them to impose a more absolute form of government. After Bathory's death many Hungarians stayed on in the Royal Guard to serve King Sigismund.

B: Ceremonial Entry of Queen Constantia; Cracow, 1605

The ceremonial entry into Cracow of the Austrian Archduchess Constantia, married by proxy to King Sigismund III of Poland, took place on 4 December 1605. It was normal in Poland to welcome foreign queens with magnificent processions in which the entire Royal Guard and numerous detachments from the nobles' private armies took part in full parade dress. The figures here are based on the famous '*Constantia Roll*'.

B1: Rotamaster of Hussars, 1605

The *rotmistrz* ('rotamaster' or captain) was the commander of a Polish cavalry troop or infantry company. He carries a *buzdygan* mace, symbol of his rank. He wears a red silk *zupan* coat, and a black furred Hungarian cap, decorated with crane or heron feathers. His swords are a Tartar-style sabre worn at the waist and a Turkish-style *koncerz*, gilded and encrusted with turquoises. He wears a single 'wing' attached to the left side of the back of the saddle, this being the most obvious place for feathered decorations after the abandonment of the wing-shaped shield also usually carried on the left side.

His Turkish parade horse is dyed half red, an Eastern fashion which aroused incredulous comments from Western observers. The English traveller Fynes Morison, in his *Itinerary* in 1598 noted that in Poland, 'They have a strange custom

Polish light cavalry, probably 'cossacks' (they are described in French sources as 'carabiniers'), from Grand Marshal Opaliński's banner under Choiński, clothed in red during the celebrated entry into Paris in 1645. Note the lack of bows and spears, and the method of slinging the carbines. Aquaforta by Stefano della Bella. (British Museum)

seeming to me ridiculous, because it is contrary to nature ... they paint their [horses'] manes, tails and the very bottoms of their bellies most subject to dirt, with a carnation colour which nature never gave to any horse ...' During a similar procession of Poles into Paris in 1645 Mme. Motteville had to admit that the fashion, 'though fantastic, was not thought unpleasing'. The pale brick-red dye was obtained from the Brasil tree, and, curiously, was guaranteed by its manufacturers to be permanent and non-toxic. The treament seems to have been reserved for light-coloured horses, though in India and Turkey darker horses were also dyed with henna. There are, in fact, even references to horses in Poland being dyed green!

B2: Hussar 'Comrade', 1605

This figure is taken from a unit on the Constantia Roll, described on a caption as the 'Royal Troop'. However, it is possible that each separate rank of this unit was based on the dress of a different hussar 'banner' that took part in the ceremony. One contemporary description of the occasion records men in the hussar 'banner' of the Castellan of Czchów, Mikolaj Spytek Ligęza, wearing red *welensy* (capes to cover armour) on which were stars and crescents, so an identification with this 'banner' seems most likely. Note that stars and crescents are common Eastern European motifs in this period. They also appear on wings, flags, mailshirts, and bowcases (see D2).

He carries a Hungarian-style sabre, and under his leg an Italian-Hungarian style *pallasz* broadsword, a variety common to the hussars and used after the lance had been broken. The stirrups are of

Haiduks and Polish light-armed cavalry attack the Swedish lines at Kircholm. The haiduks are in blocks made up of several companies, and fire from the front rank of the formation; they are all dressed in blue uniform with red trousers, black caps and shoes. The light cavalry are armed with lances, and wear curious baggy caps and shaggy wolfskins, with no uniformity in colours of dress. From the 'Battle of Kircholm' painting. (Château de Sassenage)

so-called 'Polish' type, though they owe a great deal to early Tartar models. Spurs are of the long-necked type with eight spikes, used until about the middle of the 17th century. The *szyszak* helmet is restored from an early German model of approximately similar form to the one on the roll (Wawel, Cracow). The comrade wears an *anima*-type breastplate with mail skirt and sleeves. Contemporary accounts speak of 'iron sleeves' worn with anima cuirasses, but it is not certain if this refers to separate mail sleeves, or to part of a mail shirt or to armguards. In any event, anima cuirasses of this type surviving in the Graz Armoury have separate mail skirts.

C: Polish Haiduks, 1600–25

Haiduks were the standard type of infantry in

The various types of infantry in Polish service, from a costume book by Abraham de Bruyn (1540? 87), *Habits de diverses nations . . .* published in 1581 in Antwerp, copied with slight variations from his earlier work of 1577 published in Cologne. The work was based on material supplied to de Bruyn by friends, and in his own words 'not yet known by the art of engraving or publishing'.

Poland over the period 1569–1633, and possibly even earlier. Uniformity of dress within infantry units started early in Eastern Europe—in Poland, certainly as early as 1557, and by the 1570s it was quite exceptional to find haiduks without uniform. On raising the unit an allowance was usually made for cloth for uniforms (*barwa*). NCOs and officers were usually dressed in good-quality English or Dutch woollen cloth, while the men had to settle for home-produced products. The most popular colour by far was blue in various shades, sometimes lined in red or white. Private units were dressed more or less at the whim of the commander, which usually meant in the colours of his personal badge or of the district where the men were raised.

C1: Haiduk Arquebusier
This haiduk is based closely on the '*Patterns of Costume*' painting from c.1600–25. He is armed with an arquebus, lighter than the musket which by this time was in use throughout the West but was not immediately adopted in Poland. Rather interestingly, he has no bandolier of measured charges over his shoulder. Indeed, not a single picture of Polish haiduks in this period shows bandoliers, and it seems likely that they were not used in conjunction with the arquebus. On his arm he carries a carefully wound match; over his shoulder, a canvas bag for his arquebus; and at his waist a leather bullet-pouch and a *cuir-bouilli* powder flask, of gourd shape with a flat back and fluted belly. He wears a Hungarian sabre at his waist. The typical skin-tight trousers were worn by most Poles in this period. His shoes are so-called *trzewiki*. The light axe, typical for haiduks, is not the famous *berdish*, which was of quite a different form and did not appear in large quantities until the middle of the 17th century.

C2: 'Tenth-man', Gostomski's Company, 1605

The haiduk company was organised along a decimal system, and most commonly into units of between 100 and 200 men. Each section of ten men was commanded by a non-commissioned officer (*dzięsiętnik*), who was equipped somewhat differently from the rest of his section. His uniform would often be in different colours (e.g. red lined with green rather than blue lined with red); and his chief armament was a *darda*, probably a general term for shafted weapons such as halberds, half-pikes and partisans. The odd looking partisan-spear being used here is taken from the Constantia Roll. Haiduk NCOs are often portrayed with a *darda* that looks more like a halberd. The haiduk formation drew up in ranks ten deep, so the 'tenth-man' could take his position either at front or rear. In actuality he probably changed his position depending on the tactical situation, controlling the fire of his men from the rear or second rank, and moving to the front if the formation was threatened by cavalry.

C3: Bagpiper, Stradom Town Guard, 1605

This figure is taken from a unit on the Constantia Roll, described on a caption as the Stradom Town Guard. Bagpipes, of course, were not peculiar to the Scottish Highlands; they were used widely throughout 17th-century Europe. This particular set are, however, somewhat unusual. The bag is made from a goatskin dyed pale blue, while the pipes bear more than a passing resemblance to Alpine horns; and it is easy to speculate that the location of the town of Stradom in the foothills of the Polish Highlands had some influence on the design. Other musicians used in the haiduks included drummers and fifers.

C4: Rotamaster

There were no regulations governing the dress of rotamasters, and consequently they wore rich civilian dress. There were, however, several common features in officers' dress: the large fur cap appears in several sources depicting officers, while their men are dressed only in Hungarian felt caps. Officers were also more able to afford lavish fur-lined cloaks, worn usually on the shoulders, held in place by a decorative metal brooch or chain. The rotamaster was quite often mounted. (Based on a watercolour by Heidenreich, dated 1601–12.)

Haiduks marching with an officer: a woodcut from Paprocki's book *Hetman* (1578). Paprocki probably took part in the Danzig campaign of 1577–78. Note the long skirts of the Haiduks' *delias*, tucked into their waist belts. The officer is carrying a *nadziak* war hammer with striped haft, and has a typical fur cap. (PAN Library, Kórnik)

C5: Rotamaster's Boy

There are frequent references to rotamaster's boys on haiduk company rolls; they were allowed a small wage. This one is dressed in haiduk fashion, even down to the Tartar hairstyle. The figure is based on the same source as C4. The sword is a two-hander with the arms of Mikolaj Radziwill, Voivode of Wilno dated 1572 on the blade, now in the Museum für Deutsche Geschichte in East Berlin. Several pictorial sources show the young servants of Polish officers carrying such swords, despite their very un-Eastern appearance.

D1: Light-armed cavalryman, first quarter of the 17th century

Based on the contemporary painting of the battle of Kircholm, this could represent the appearance of unarmoured 'cossacks', Tartars, or rear ranks of hussar formations. Wolfskin cloaks were more common than leopardskins, and were worn by 'comrades' as well as 'retainers'. One incident confirming the wearing of wolfskins occurred prior to the battle of Kircholm in 1605, when a Lithuanian hussar was captured in battle gear and wolfskin by the Swedes, and taken to the Swedish King Charles IX. Count Mansfeld, one of the more distinguished of the Swedish officers, reportedly said to Charles: 'If all the Poles are like this one, I do not doubt that they will stand and fight our army'.

This praise infuriated Charles, who at once replied: 'Go dress yourself in a wolfskin, and you'll be just as frightening'. (Naruszewicz, History of J. K. Chodkiewicz, 1781.)

The cap, reconstructed from the Kircholm painting, seems to have been influenced greatly by the Serbian *deli's* cap, as shown on contemporary sources (Codex Vindobonensis, c.1590). It is well known that the Polish nobility tried to imitate Tartar fashions; this new piece of evidence would suggest that they also tried to imitate the Serbian *deli*.

D2: Polish 'Cossack' cavalry officer, 1600–25

The *misiurka* mail helmet was often replaced by a rather more comfortable, typically Polish fur cap derived from the Tartar *kuczma*, and worn both summer and winter. Such caps were widely worn on campaign by 'cossacks' as well as hussars: and most contemporary pictures of the battle of Vienna show cavalry in fur caps rather than metal helmets.

The figure is taken as closely as possible from the 'Patterns of Costumes' painting, which can in fact be dated largely from the equipment worn on this figure alone. He carries a wheel-lock *bandolet* carbine (reconstructed from an example in the Polish Army Museum) and the typical Oriental

bowcase and early short quiver. The figure is very similar to an engraving in Abraham Boot's *Journael van der Legatie* from 1627. His sword is very similar to a gilded eagle-head sabre belonging to Christian II, Elector of Saxony, from 1610, now in the Historical Museum, Dresden, and has been restored from this. The armguard on the left arm seems to be of a Western style. This also supports the dating of the picture to the early 17th century since the Oriental *karvash* armguard was—according to Bochenski—only gradually introduced in Poland over the first decades of the 17th century. The rich dress and lack of an armguard on the right would tend to suggest that this man is an officer—Polish officers frequently rode into battle with their right forearm bared as a mark of command.

D3 & D4: Peasant infantry, 1630s

Based on watercolours added to one copy of Abraham Boot's *Journael* . . . (Gdansk Archives), these figures must give a fairly good idea of the appearance of ununiformed peasant levies, such as the *Wybraniecka* infantry, throughout much of the 17th century. They wear clothes made from sheepskins and homespun cloth and linen. They were rarely expected to take part in combat, and so were often specifically required not to have weapons or uniform. Tools and field-obstacles are added from the contemporary MS. of Naronowicz-Naroński's *Military Architecture*.

E1: Polish Cavalryman, c.1640

The dress of a nobleman, and therefore 'undress'

Gostomski's haiduk company, 1605. It numbers 100 men, organised in ten ranks of ten. The front rank is of *dziesiętniks* ('tenth-men'), armed with a *darda* (halberd or partisan) on which is a pennant; behind these are nine ranks of arquebusiers, all uniformly equipped and dressed. The flag is red with a white cross. Rather interestingly the mounted officer is dressed in a mail shirt and leopardskin. From the Constantia Roll. (Royal Castle, Warsaw)

42

uniform of 'armoured cossacks' or hussars, or combat dress of unarmoured cossacks. He has many typically Polish features. Note the form of the fur cap. Colours here have been restored from general accounts of Polish dress: poorer noblemen often wore blue colours, and by the beginning of the 18th century this seems to have developed into the uniform colour for light cavalry. (Based on the relief in Tarłów church.)

The various types of war-hammers (*czekan*, *nadziak* and *obuch*) have been commonly identified as insignia of rank distinguishing lieutenants, though this appears to be going beyond the evidence: the war-hammer was carried by any nobleman who felt so inclined, and on occasion by entire units of cavalry during parades. Visitors to Poland mention that war-hammers were commonly used as walking sticks (as here) and to keep the arm in trim for using the sword. On several occasions laws were passed to prevent carrying of war-hammers in public, because of the terrible wounds they caused in brawls. This seems to have influenced the development of the *obuch*, a variant of the *nadziak* with the spike bent back. In combat, however, soldiers seem to have preferred the sword.

E2: Pancerni 'cossack', late 17th century
By the second half of the 17th century the *pancerni* were the all-purpose cavalry. This man wears a *karabela* sword of combat variety, an item which was just coming into fashion. He carries a *bandolet* (carbine) slung over his back, and an assortment of pistols in holsters or, as contemporaries frequently mention, tucked into waist belts. Note the twist of straw worn round the body; this was a field sign to distinguish the *pancerni* and light cavalry from Turkish *sipahi*-type cavalry and Tartars. He has many Eastern items: *kalkan* shield, bowcase and *karvash* armguards.

In Lithuania the *petyhorcy* formations carried a 2.5m long *rohatyna* (lance). In 1654 suggestions were put forward to extend the use of the lance to the whole of the Crown army because of their high value against the Muscovites; this, apparently, was never carried out. However, before the Turkish war of 1672 there was considerable discussion among such worthies as military theorist Fredro and Hetman Sobieski about the introduction of the lance to all of the Crown cavalry and to the Levy of

Haiduk from the *Wzorzec Ubiorów* ('Patterns of Costume') oil painting by an unknown artist, showing the dress of civilians and soldiers around 1600–25. This picture is particularly interesting because it shows the full equipment carried by a haiduk. (Gołuchów Castle)

the Nobility. As a result, in 1673, some *pancerni* units were armed with a *dzida* (short lance) 1.8 to 2.0 metres long; and by 1676 most Crown *pancerni* units had received them.

F: Turkish Wars, 1672–83
F1: Hussar Comrade
The helmet and face mask is from a rather unusual example in the Fitzwilliam Museum, Cambridge. It is dated to around 1640, though the mask may have been added several decades later. The body armour is of a type used from about the 1630s onwards. His swords are a hussar sabre with fully closed bow on the hilt; and the Hungarian style

43

Polish haiduks: a watercolour in a Danzig heraldic album by Michael Heidenreich, dated 1601–12. Leading are two officers; behind these are men dressed entirely in blue (one red) with small black caps, and a boy, dressed in green, carrying an officer's two-hand sword. (PAN Library, Kórnik)

koncerz, a long piercing sword of triangular or square section. Many Western items were beginning to creep into hussar equipment during the second half of the 17th century. Note, for instance, the simple stirrups and spurs. The horse furniture is restored from an example in the Polish Army Museum.

The pair of 'wings' consist of a wooden frame, fringed with red velvet, edged in brass, into which are placed a single row of feathers. Current research suggests that wings of this type were not worn on the back until after the first quarter of the 17th century. Contemporary accounts are contradictory about the use of wings in pairs or singly; some state that 'comrades' wore wings while their retainers did not, other state that only retainers wore them. It is specifically mentioned in a commission of 1576 that wings and similar feathered ornaments should be worn as the rotamaster thought appropriate. This suggests that the use of wings varied from 'banner' to 'banner', though was largely uniform among men of equal rank within a unit.

The lance pennant is based on seven identical surviving examples in the Polish Army Museum.

The lance decoration is restored from the haft of a Polish standard in the Swedish Trophy collection.

Our hussar is riding down a Turkish Janissary.

G: Moldavian, Wallachian and Hungarian Campaigns, 1685–91

The success of the Vienna campaign did little to improve the situation of Poland: 'As useful as fighting for Vienna' even became a metaphor for a fruitless venture. Sobieski sent several expeditions to what are now Rumania and Hungary, and each in its turn was less successful than the one before. The Turkish Wars did, however, have a major impact on fashion in Poland. Diarists mention the huge quantity of Turkish booty circulating in Poland after the Chocim and Vienna campaigns; and since the supply was obviously limited, and everyone in Poland wanted to give the impression that they, too, had fought in the campaigns, workshops were overloaded with production of imitation Oriental goods.

Also in this period 'Sarmatism' began to have a greater influence on fashion. The Poles, probably looking at armour influenced by the Scythians and Sarmatians, whom they regarded as their ancestors, began to copy patterns that had, in turn, been copied from the classical Greeks. (See, for example

Scythian Gorgon plaques in MAA 137, *The Scythians*.) The 'Gorgon's head' devices worn as ornamental brass plaques bear a striking resemblance to classical Greek emblems, while the scale armour points clearly to Scythian and Sarmatian models.

G1: Grand Hetman of the Crown (1682–1702), Stanislaw Jablonowski

As Grand Hetman of the Crown, Jablonowski commanded a wing of the Polish army at Vienna, though in Sobieski's absence he was full commander-in-chief. After Vienna he began to show a much greater influence on the development of the army. His main claim to fame is that in 1688/9, in an attempt to reform the ailing Polish army, he committed a crime which has unfairly scarred his name in the memories of generations of Poles: he took away the lance from the hussars in the field. This was, at the time, the only possible method of trying to reform the hussars who, though costing a substantial proportion of the ever-decreasing money available, were of little value in the burn-and-run warfare of the Wallachian and Hungarian campaigns after Vienna.

In Poland 'Sarmatian' scale armour is known as *karacena*, a word derived from the Italian *corazzina*, (a type of scale armour). *Karacena* was made of metal scales sewn onto elkskin or deerskin backing or riveted onto a metal base, and made up into suits of hussar-style armour. It was extremely expensive to produce, and was worn only by wealthy officers. Because of the poor protective qualities of the armour compared to normal plate, it was often worn over mail. It is still not entirely clear if it was used in combat, though certain features—such as the Gorgon's head plaques—undoubtedly were. References to the appearance of *karacena* occur as early as 1637, though it does not seem to have made a major impact until after the Vienna campaign; it was still being worn in the 1760s. The superb *karacena* armours of the later period are regarded by many as the high point of Polish armour-making.

The armour (National Museum, Cracow), thumb-ring sabre (Czartoryski Collection, Cracow), and mace (Jasnogóra Treasure-House, Częstochowa) all once belonged to Jablonowski. Gorgon's head plaques, which are missing from the armour, have been restored from the armour of Field Hetman Sieniawski. The method of wearing the leopard skin has been restored from his portrait. The Turkish saddle was captured at Vienna by Hetman Sieniawski. Stirrups are of Turkish style, and all furniture is profusely decorated with turquoises, a favourite in the East, where turquoises were believed to act as talismans against wounds in battle.

G2: Bunczuk Bearer

The armour he wears is a fairly unusual example of mixed mail and scale in the collection at Kórnik in Poland. His sabre is an early example of the *karabela*, a classic Polish style (though originally based on Turkish models). It became the standard dress sword, worn in Poland well into the 19th century (Kórnik Collections, Nr.2102).

The standard he carries is a *bunczuk*; developed

Field-obstacles: (1) 'iron stakes'; (2) and (3) mobile 'chevaux de frise'; (4) and (5) abattis; (5) bis, iron caltrops scattered in the anticipated line of an attack. From MS. copy of *Budownictwo Woiennego* ('Military Architecture') by Narońowicz-Naroński (1659). (Warsaw Univ. Libr.)

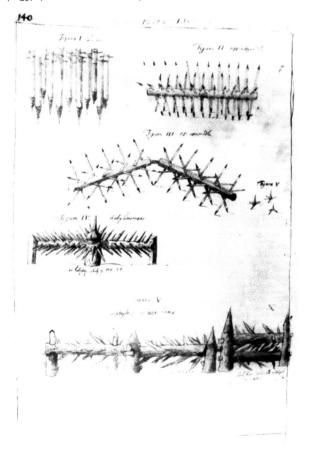

from Turkish horse-tail standards, *tugs*, they were carried mainly by hetmen, though the king also used them. In the presence of the king, the hetmen were supposed to lower their own *buńczuks* in respect. The bearer (who held the special rank of *buńczuczny*) is perhaps from a *pancerni* 'banner'; Sobieski, for example, had a 200-strong *pancerni* 'banner' to guard his own *buńczuk*. In Polish usage *buńczuks* varied considerably in style, but there would seem to have been a tendency towards using wing devices rather than horse-tails. It has also been suggested that a cap was placed on the gilded wooden ball on the top of the *buńczuk*. This is not certain, though these caps must have been attached by some means to the lance-heads of hetman's insignia. This particular example is based on a *buńczuk* traditionally belonging to a hetman of the Lubomirski family. Note in particular the use of painted feathers on the highly decorative hussar-style lance. Erratum: the standard should be c. 5m long, its ball c. 12cm across.

H1: Banner of the District of Grodno, Lithuania

Used on ceremonial occasions and by the General Levy of the Nobility when called out for war, this flag dates from the reign of Sigismund III, 1587–1632. The cloth is single-sided, very ornately patterned damask silk, each colour being made from a different piece of cloth sewn *in intarsia*. The numerous repairs made to the original flag would suggest that it had a very long life, probably until the end of the Republic in 1795. Some of the repairs have left the flag badly disfigured; the illustration here is a reconstruction of the most probable original form, with a single pointed tail, made on the basis of a surviving flag of the same type, and of 19th-century drawings by Lesser. The rider in the badge in the hoist is the *Vytis* (rider), heraldic symbol of Lithuania, known in Poland as the *Pogón* ('pursuit'). In the fly is a rosette with the word 'GRODZIENSKA' (from Grodno). Other Lithuanian flags of this series from Sigismund's reign are known: the flag of the *powiat* (district) of Slonim is in the Polish Army museum, while flags of the district of Wolkowysk and the palatinate of Troki (two-tailed) were in Polish collections in the 19th century. The flags of this series are all of similar design, but of differing colours. Dimensions: 196 × c.300cm reconstructed fly. (MWP, 3058*.)

H2: Banner of the Court Army of King Sigismund III, 1621

The appearance of this flag was noted by a Swedish agent in Lublin in October 1621. It was being carried at the head of the Royal Hussar troop, which he reported was composed of about 500 volunteer noblemen in great splendour (Riksarkivet, Stockholm, M.1290). It bears the heraldic Polish eagle and white cross devices on a deep crimson field. The central badge is the wheatsheaf of the Vasa family; around the eagle is the chain of the Order of the Golden Fleece. The inscription translates as '*With Thee and for Thee*'. The silk flag is double-sided, with ornamentation in embroidery and appliqué. In 1655 it was captured in Warsaw by the Swedes and taken into their trophy collection. Dimensions: 282 × 288cm. (ST:28:4.)

Turkish tents, part of the booty taken at Vienna and used by the Polish army afterwards. Such quantities of these were taken that many were simply torn up for rags on the march back to Poland. From the Melk sketchbook of the Italian painter Martino Altomonte, court painter of Sobieski, commissioned from 1684 to produce pictures of his great battles. (Benediktinerstift, Melk, Austria)

H3: Standard of 'Cossack' troop commanded by Jan Slawinski, Sword-Bearer of Starodub, Lithuania

Starodub was at the very edge of Polish dominions close to Muscovy at the date indicated on the flag: 1649. The Archangel Michael, in particular, hints at the Orthodox religion of the levying area. This and the other decorations are painted on both sides of the silk flag. The reverse differs slightly: instead of scales, the Archangel carries a small pennon, and there is no date. The flag has all the ingredients typical of Polish-Lithuanian flags of the period: Knight's Cross, picture of a religious patron, and the arms of the rotamaster surrounded by abbreviations of his name and titles: I(an) S(lawinski) M(iecznik) S(tarodubski). The double-headed arrow device is the badge called in Poland *Kozieglowa*, often used in Lithuania without a name (Niesiecki's *Herbarz*, t.I, p. 562). Dimensions: 104 × 110cm. (MWP, 565*.)

H4: Personal Standard of Hetman or Grand-Marshal, first half of the 17th century

Made of patterned European silk damask with wing *in intarsia*, the flag was captured by the Swedes some time before 1660. The winged claw device has been identified as the '*Topacz*' heraldic badge, though if this were the case the wing should be black and without the heart. There were several notable soldiers bearing the Topacz badge, the most distinguished being Szymon Kopyciński, who commanded a Royal hussar troop in the period 1611–30. It seems, however, that the winged claw is not just a heraldic badge, but a military symbol which came into Polish use from connections with Hungary, Rumania and Serbia. Similar flags were noted, for instance at Chocim in 1621 when the hussar troop of the Lithuanian Hetman Chod-kiewicz lost a great white standard on which was a black eagle's wing, one he had reportedly had with him for at least ten years. In 1646 Queen Marie-Louise de Gonzague's entries into Gdansk and Warsaw were opened by a 'cossack' unit belonging to Grand-Marshal Opaliński, carrying a red standard with a black and yellow winged claw. Taking this into account, it seems that winged claw flags were used as personal standards, carried by bodyguards of commanding officers. The possible connection here with later winged *buńczuk* standards is also interesting (see F2). Dimensions 148 × 240cm. (ST: 29:123.)

Royal Standard of King John Sobieski. It has a cream border and red central field fringed in gold and embroidered in silver. The silver Polish eagle has on its breast Sobieski's *Janina* badge (a curved shield) in silver on a blue cartouche outlined in gold. (Astronomers may be interested to note that this is the shield referred to in the constellation 'Scutum Sobieskii'.) The reverse has instead of the eagle the silver outline of a Knight's Cross. The cloth has been dated by textile experts to the 17th century; and an account of Sobieski's coronation in 1676 (Ossolinski MS.337) describes an embroidered flag with eagle and blue shield carried by the Crown Standard Bearer. Though this does not identify the flag with certainty, standards of very similar design are known to have been carried by the personal escorts of later Polish monarchs. (Wilanów 3790, Warsaw)

INDEX

(References to illustrations are shown in **bold**. Plates are also shown in **bold**, with caption locators in brackets.)

Contents

Introduction

It is many years since Froebel,[1] followed by American educator Caroline Pratt,[2] focussed their research on the value of the 'unit block' and block building in the development and learning of young children.

Today, block play continues to offer a vast range of experiences for children. From an early age it encourages creativity, sensitivity to others and sharing, as well as supporting communication and language development.

Practitioners working with young children also observe improvement in self-control, fine and large muscle control, and of motor skills such as lifting, stacking and balancing.

Block building is a developmental process; progressing as the child discovers and applies new possibilities. Other advantages are the natural exposure to counting, and the observation of similarities and differences in shapes, sizes and amounts.

For older children, block play becomes the doorway to the discovery of mathematics, technology, engineering and even architecture. A prime example of this is Frank Lloyd Wright,[3] whose decision to be an architect was shaped by playing with building blocks as a child.

With guidance from the practitioner, children can learn to create, to imagine, to bounce ideas off each other and to think for themselves.

The aim of this guide is to help practitioners working with children in the Early Years Foundation Stage make the most of block play opportunities.

[1] Educator Friedrich Froebel (1782–1852) designed the educational play materials known as Froebel Gifts or Fröbelgaben, which included geometric building blocks and pattern activity blocks.

[2] Caroline Pratt designed the wooden unit blocks that became a basic material in schools across the United States. Her standard unit block is the same shape as the blocks of the fourth Froebel Gift based on the proportions 1:2:4. Other blocks were derived from this standard block, some smaller and others larger as described by Froebel in *The Education of Man* published in 1826.

[3] Frank Lloyd Wright (born Frank Lincoln Wright, 1867–1959) was an American (of Welsh descent) architect, interior designer, writer and educator.

The power and value of block play as a tool for learning and thinking

We need to explore the reason why blocks are so powerful. We begin to understand this by looking at some of the characteristics of quality play provision.

Key features of quality play provisions include resources that are:

- open ended;
- adaptable;
- versatile;
- long-lasting;
- have limitless possibilities in use;
- timeless;
- safe.

Blocks have all these features. But, besides being unique, they are also:

- a system designed to be logical and mathematically precise;
- a means of symbolic representation;
- a medium for non-verbal communication, which also supports the development of verbal communication.

Block play as a tool for learning

Blocks reflect many values closely related to young children's development and learning, so that through block play they are able to:

- be themselves;
- explore, experiment, investigate and problem solve;

harness their imaginative powers with their own creative ideas and thinking;

gain satisfaction from being actively involved in explorations and investigations;

gain independence and control over their learning, to keep their interest and develop their creativity;

test things out, practice and solve problems without risk of failure;

create in 3D and represent ideas symbolically;

extend their learning (blocks allow for differentiated learning) making decisions based on thinking things through in a logical way;

enhance physical, intellectual, linguistic, social and emotional areas of development;

develop concentration through engagement and motivation;

develop a sense of achievement and increased self-esteem and confidence, as there is no right and wrong way of building with blocks.[3]

Block play as a tool for thinking

A set of blocks is made up of different shapes, which work together as a system. Individual blocks can be put together to make infinite arrangements.

Blocks were originally designed to be used as a system on their own. It is still a good idea to introduce them to children like this, giving them time to become familiar with the different shapes before introducing other resources, which may then lead them into more complex play as they begin to extend their thoughts and ideas.

Just as a building is not complete until it is finished and being used, so children's play goes through a similar process. This will sometimes take the form of decorating their creations with fabric and natural objects, such as shells and pebbles. They may choose to build on their own experiences or enter into the realms of imaginary play by incorporating small figures, animals or vehicles into their block play.

Having an easily accessible range of open-ended resources available will enable children to take their play in the direction they want it to go.

Being familiar with the various block forms can help us to understand and interpret young children's thinking. Many of these basic forms can be linked to schemas (patterns of thinking behaviour). For example: trajectory or straight lines, rotation, connecting, enveloping and transporting.

A young child will begin by carrying their blocks around. This evolves into planning and constructing buildings or objects they have seen and know, and eventually to creations of their imagination.

These are often dramatised, with different blocks becoming symbols representing characters and settings.

³ Refer to The Early Years Foundation Stage video clip on the CD for Card 4:2 Learning and Development – Active Learning. This shows a small group of children working together on a large block construction, and afterwards their work in progress is cordoned off, showing that their achievement is valued and respected. (DCSF Publications, The Early Years Foundation Stage [2007] www.everychildmatters.gov.uk)

Stages in block play

Educators have observed that all children seem to pass through established stages when block building, whether it is introduced to them at the age of 2 or 6.

The speed at which a child passes through these stages depends on the amount of time he or she has been exposed to block play.

Even an older child coming into contact with block building for the first time will begin at the earliest stages, perhaps moving more quickly through them until catching up to the stage that others of his or her age may be in.

In her book *The Art of Block Building* (1966) Harriet Merrill Johnson has listed these stages:

Stage 1 Blocks are carried around, but not used for construction. This applies to the very young child, under 2 years of age.

Stage 2 At approximately age 2 or 3, building begins. Children mostly make rows on the floor horizontally or vertically (stacking).

Stage 3 Bridging – two blocks with a space between them, connected by a third block.

Stage 4 Enclosures – four blocks placed in such a way that they enclose a space.

Stage 5 Patterns and symmetry are to be observed in building. Buildings are not generally named (approx age 3-4 years).

Stage 6 Naming of structures for dramatic play, with names that relate to the function of the building (approx age 4-5 years).

Stage 7 Block building often reproduces actual structures known by children. There is a strong impulse for dramatic play around the structure (approx age 5 years).

Basic block forms

Behaviour patterns in block play[4]

"When we observe children, we see, as Froebel began to see last century, and theory and research has shown this century, that there is some patterning in their behaviour."

(Gura & Bruce, 1992)

While building with blocks children may be observed creating some of the following:

- building towers upwards (verticals);
- building along in rows (horizontals);
- making slopes;
- making enclosures – circular, square or linear (regular or irregular);
- edge bordering;
- filling in;
- making a central core with radials, or zigzag lines, or intersections or grids;
- making symmetrical or asymmetrical forms;
- putting blocks inside, outside, over, under, on, through, rotating;
- transporting blocks from here to there and back.

[4]Adapted from the Froebel Blockplay Research Video (1992)

Basic block patterns[5]

1-dimensional – Linear

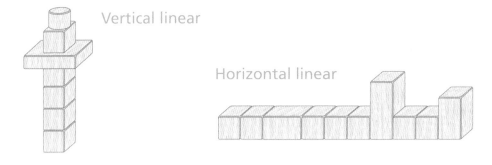

Vertical linear

Horizontal linear

1-dimensional – Areal

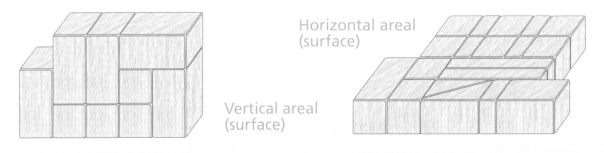

Horizontal areal
(surface)

Vertical areal
(surface)

3-dimensional – Volumetric

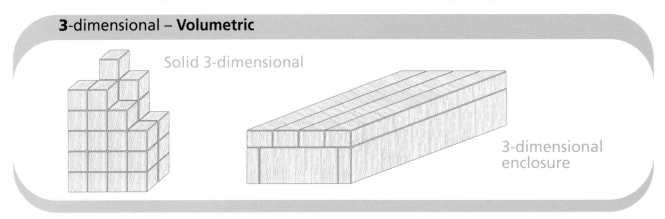

Solid 3-dimensional

3-dimensional
enclosure

2-dimensional – **Enclosure**

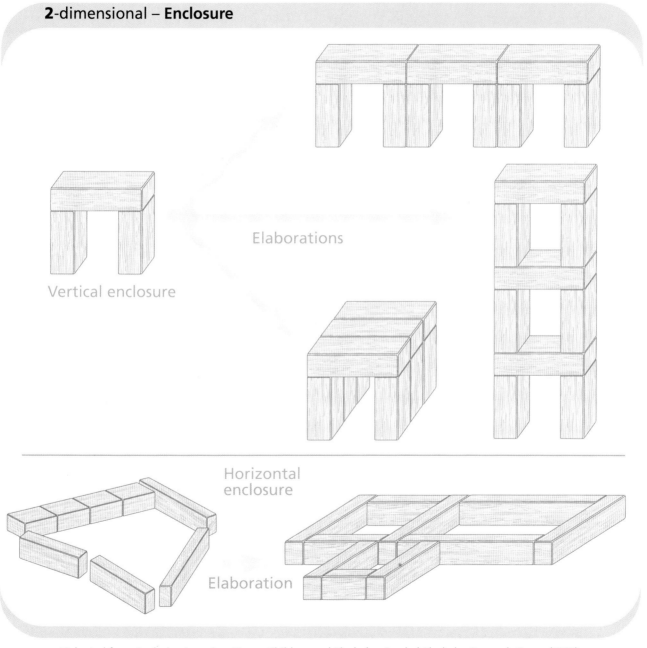

Vertical enclosure

Elaborations

Horizontal enclosure

Elaboration

[5]Adapted from *Exploring Learning: Young Children and Blockplay*, Froebel Blockplay Research Group (1992).

Block play and the Early Years Foundation Stage

Block play provides a vast range of experiences for children across the Early Years Foundation Stage. It offers opportunities to develop young children's learning in all areas:

Personal, Social and Emotional Development

Block play helps develop:

- communication;

- collaboration;

- negotiation;

- understanding of rules and considerate behaviour;

- risk-taking;

- confidence;

- making choices and decisions;

- concentration;

- leadership;

- anticipation;

- problem solving.[6]

[6]Refer to the Early Years Foundation Stage Framework CD video clip for effective planning and resourcing, to develop disposition and attitude, (developmental matters 40–60 months), which shows a practitioner supporting children in a challenging but achievable task of putting the blocks away. (DCSF Publications, The Early Years Foundation Stage [2007] www.everychildmatters.gov.uk)

Communication, Language and Literacy Development

Block play helps to develop:

- communication;
- relevant vocabulary;
- imagination;
- drama;
- story-making;
- representation of own ideas and symbols;
- mark-making.

Problem Solving, Reasoning and Numeracy

Block play helps young children learn about:

- sorting, matching, order, sequence, counting, comparison;
- measurement – space, size, length, mass;
- shape – form, angles, symmetry;
- fractions – units, halves, quarters;
- position;
- patterns and relationships (tessellation);
- mathematical vocabulary;
- representation and recording;
- estimating.

Knowledge and Understanding of the World

Block play helps children learn about:

- different properties – balance, weight, fit, support, stability, structures, design, problem solving, testing;

- different building structures;

- human interaction with the environment such as road systems and bridges;

- mapping and representation.

Physical Development

Block play helps develop:

- motor skills;

- control;

- use of space;

- judgement;

- collaboration;

- understanding that equipment has to be used and stored safely.

Creative Development

Block play helps develop:

- exploration;

- expression and communication of ideas, thoughts and feelings;

- imaginative and creative ideas;

- aesthetic awareness;

- development of 3D structures. [7]

[7]For ideas on open-ended play refer to *I made a unicorn! Open-ended play with blocks and simple materials* available to download from: www.communityplaythings.co.uk

Organisation and
management of block play

To make block play work it is important to give careful consideration to how the activity is organised and managed. A self-selection workshop area is ideal.

Considerations for a block play area

Siting the area – establish a designated area

If possible a corner is best as it provides less danger of demolition due to passing traffic. This can be achieved by using low pieces of furniture, such as the block shelf or low storage units. This provides security and also allows clear visibility. Settings that do not have their own premises and need to pack away each day, should try to set aside a designated area away from the busiest part of the room, along with wheeled storage for the blocks.

Time and space – all important in planning block play

If you only have a short amount of time, don't attempt block play. You need to allow time for children to become engrossed and absorbed in what they are doing.

Children need time for sustained concentration, which gives them room to develop their play, process it in their minds and return to it later or even the next day. Children will not necessarily have finished an activity just because it is time to pack away.

A large space is also vital if children are to have the opportunity to physically extend their ideas. Block play needs a flat, soft surface indoors or out. A large piece of carpet is ideal.

Whenever possible, let the child save his or her creation at the end of the day. This builds enthusiasm. However, due to the size of the block play creations, this is not always possible. Encourage older children to make a quick sketch or take a digital photograph. This can be displayed in the area or given to the child to take home.

Storage

Open shelving is ideal as the blocks are easily accessible to the children. Shelves can be labelled with the name and photograph of each type of block stored there, so children know where they belong when it is time to tidy up. See Appendix 3 for labels for block play storage.

Displays

Try the following ideas:

  display pictures and photographs of different buildings and structures;

  display photographs of the children's constructions;

  record children's verbal comments and 2D representations, for example drawings, paintings and collages.

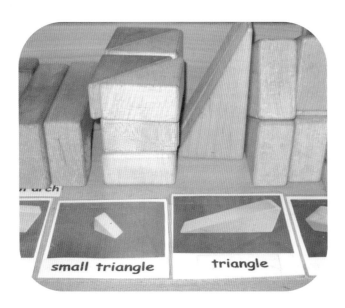

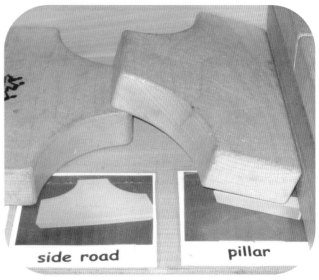

Other considerations

Resources

Have enough blocks to provide a system and avoid frustration for the children.

Tidying-up

Give 10- and 5-minute time warnings before it is time to stop. Children are not conscious of time. Tidying-up quickly and in an orderly way is a skill. Use the opportunity to teach children to put blocks back on the storage shelves in an orderly way, matching them to the relevant photographs, with the heaviest and largest blocks lowest, and each kind kept together.

Boundaries (rules)

The practitioner needs to establish basic rules for block play with regard to safety, sensitivity to others and respect for the resources.

Including parents in block play

Parents can be involved in a number of ways:

- displays;

- workshops;

- involving them in their own observations of their child (these can be written observations or photographs from home, which are then shared with their child's Key Person);

- linking up block play with the local environment, such as local buildings and structures, to raise awareness;

- invite parents to join walks in the local environment to look at different types of buildings, structures and roads.

The role of the adult in developing block play

The adult's role in block play is of vital importance: to know their children and to quietly observe.

Adult involvement

Each child has different needs that often surface in block play. The presence of an adult in the block play area, down on the floor with the children whenever possible, will build their enthusiasm. Partnering children in block play allows the adult to:

- be an enthusiastic bystander, observing closely what the children are doing;

- recognise when they should observe and when to get involved;

- give support while, importantly, allowing the children to take the lead (do not take over or dominate what they are doing);

- develop relevant language.

By quietly being aware and part of their play the adult is able to support the children to be focussed and happy.

The adult's role in the language of blocks

It is important for practitioners to be clear and consistent about the words that they want to introduce to the children. Providing opportunities to talk will allow children to develop their understanding of how to use new words in different situations. This also applies to block play.

When researchers in the Froebel Blockplay Research Project named the blocks they, "wanted to avoid, as far as possible, a vocabulary that might influence both our own perceptions of the child's purpose and the uses to which blocks might be put if such terms as 'cross roads' block and 'bridge' block were adopted" (Gura & Bruce, 1992).

Therefore the advice from the researchers is that practitioners within a school or setting should consult each other and agree appropriate use of block language to ensure continuity with shared terms and meanings. (For illustrations and names of individual blocks see Appendices 1 and 2.)

Summary
Bibliography
Appendices
Acknowledgements

Summary

The value of block play is such that it touches every area of learning and every area of child development.

As a developmental process it offers a vast range of experiences, which allow children to discover, refine and extend their learning.

Playing with blocks can even lay the foundations for developing skills that will be valuable in later life. But, above all, because building with blocks is open-ended, there can be no wrong method or outcome. Therefore, children can develop confidence and the freedom to explore, create and lead their own learning.

Bibliography

Community Playthings (n.d.) *Foundations: The value of block play,* CD-ROM, available from: www.communityplaythings.co.uk

Community Products (UK) Limited (2008) *I made a unicorn! Open-ended play with blocks and simple materials*, available to download from: www.communityplaythings.co.uk

DCSF (2008) *The Early Years Foundation Stage (EYFS) Pack May 2008, DCSF-00261-2008, available from: http://nationalstrategies.standards.dcsf.gov.uk/earlyyears http://publications.teachernet.gov.uk*

Gura, P. (ed. with the Froebel Blockplay Research Group directed by Tina Bruce) (1992) *Exploring Learning, Young Children and Blockplay,* London: Paul Chapman Publishing Ltd.

Hirsch, E. (1996) *The Block Book (3rd edition),* Washington, DC: NAEYC.

Johnson, H. (1966) Reprinted from *The Art of Block Building,* by Harriet Merrill Johnson, originally published in 1933 by The John Day Company, copyright by Bank Street College of Education.

Appendix 1: Unit blocks

Adapted from Community Playthings: **www.communityplaythings.co.uk**

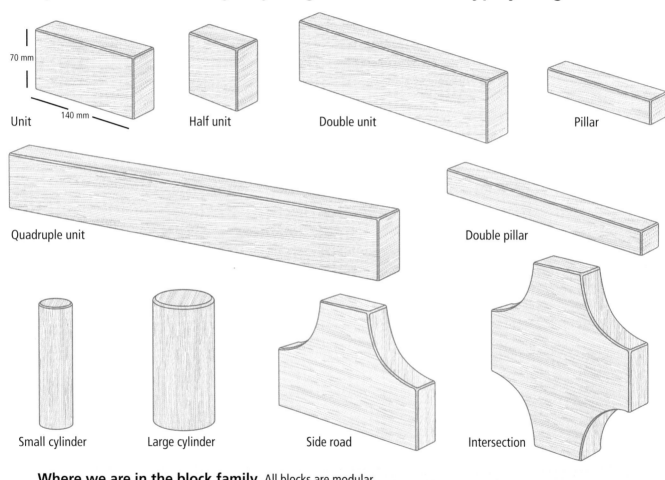

70 mm

Unit   140 mm

Half unit

Double unit

Pillar

Quadruple unit

Double pillar

Small cylinder

Large cylinder

Side road

Intersection

Where we are in the block family. All blocks are modular.

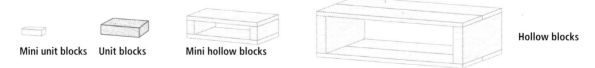

Mini unit blocks   Unit blocks   Mini hollow blocks

Hollow blocks

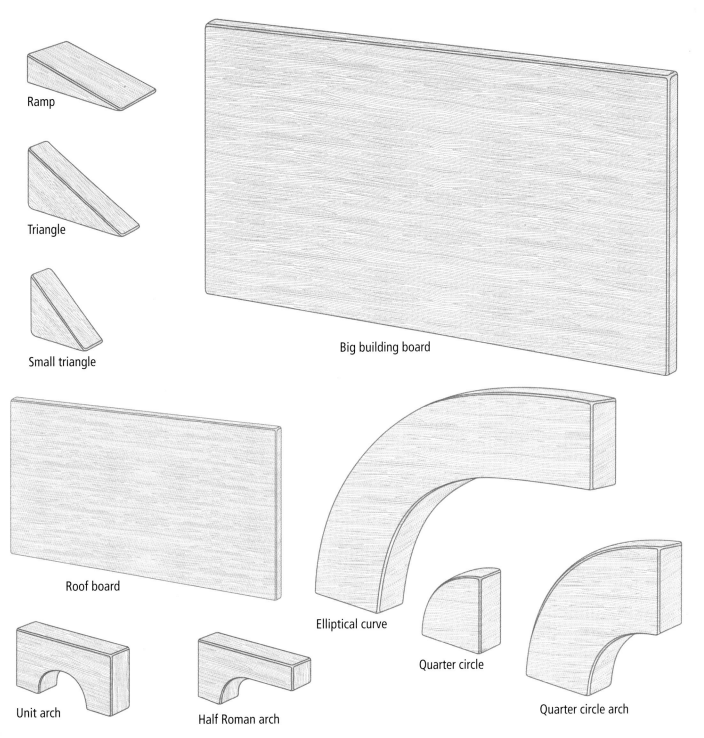

Ramp

Triangle

Small triangle

Big building board

Roof board

Elliptical curve

Quarter circle

Quarter circle arch

Unit arch

Half Roman arch

31

Appendix 2: Hollow blocks

Adapted from Community Playthings: **www.communityplaythings.co.uk**

Half square
14 x 14 x 28 cm
Soild hardwood, screwed joints, weather-resistant finish.

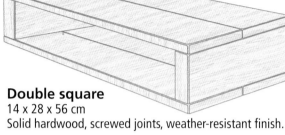

Double square
14 x 28 x 56 cm
Solid hardwood, screwed joints, weather-resistant finish.

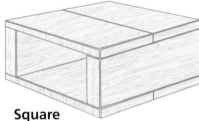

Square
14 x 28 x 28 cm
Solid hardwood, screwed joints, weather-resistant finish.

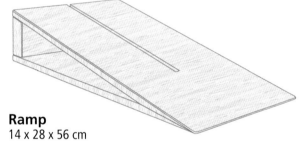

Ramp
14 x 28 x 56 cm
Solid hardwood, screwed joints, weather-resistant finish.

Short board
10 cm x 56 cm x 14 mm
Solid hardwood, weather-resistant finish.

Long board
14 cm x 112 cm x 19 mm
Solid hardwood, weather-resistant finish.

Where we are in the block family. All blocks are modular.

Mini unit blocks   Unit blocks

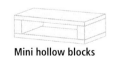

Mini hollow blocks

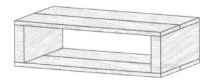

Hollow blocks

Appendix 3:
Unit block classification for storage labelling

You can photocopy and laminate the following labels and use them with photographs of individual blocks for storage labelling. See page 22 for an example of a storage system for blocks.

unit

half unit

double unit

quadruple unit

pillar

ramp

triangle

small triangle

unit arch

half roman arch

big building board

small cylinder

large cylinder

side road

intersection

roof board

elliptical curve

quarter circle arch

quarter circle

double pillar

NOTES: